Nicely Said

WRITING FOR THE WEB WITH STYLE AND PURPOSE

Nicole Fenton and Kate Kiefer Lee

NICELY SAID
Writing for the Web with Style and Purpose

Nicole Fenton and Kate Kiefer Lee

Peachpit Press
www.peachpit.com

To report errors, please send a note to errata@peachpit.com
Peachpit Press is a division of Pearson Education

Project Editor: Nancy Peterson
Production Editor: Tracey Croom
Development Editor: Margaret S. Anderson/Stellarvisions
Copyeditor: Gretchen Dykstra
Proofers: Liz Welch, Gretchen Dykstra
Compositor: Kim Scott/Bumpy Design
Indexer: Rebecca Plunkett
Cover Design: Alvin Diec
Interior Design: Kim Scott/Bumpy Design

ISBN 13: 978-0-321-98819-5

ISBN 10:   0-321-98819-1

9 8 7 6 5 4 3 2 1

Printed and bound in the United States of America

CONTENTS

FOREWORD

IF YOU'RE NOT A PROFESSIONAL WRITER, The Fear usually strikes early: either at the very idea of needing to write, or at the moment when it's time to begin typing and the terror of the blank page leaps up and freezes your hands on the keyboard. Many (most?) professional writers feel the same thing, along with bonus terrors near the midpoint of a project ("Why did I ever agree to this?!") and at the very end ("This is probably completely incomprehensible and I can't even tell anymore").

Much of that fear arises because our task is so unclear. Writing is something we're rarely taught, beyond mechanics and a little instruction about the five-paragraph essay. But writing—especially in a business context—is a craft with principles and methods that have little to do with grammar and mechanics and everything to do with identifying and meeting readerly needs. Even if they don't realize it, experienced writers understand and rely on those principles and methods, but it's very difficult to find introductions or explanations that deal with them head-on.

That's the first reason this book is such a joy. Whether you write full-time for a big agency or juggle a dozen hats at a tiny nonprofit or startup, this book will give you starting points, help with common web writing questions, and most importantly, a *coherent and repeatable approach to writing*. In the chapters that follow, you'll find step-by-step guidance through the stages of research, writing, and revision, as well as detailed advice on developing a lively, appropriate voice and tone. You'll also find in-depth discussions of dozens of weird little problems that trip up even the most experienced writers: things like handling the corporate "we"/"us" without sounding creepy, using humor without alienating readers, and navigating the strangely worded waters of legal copy. (And the chapter on clear, ethical, humane marketing is worth the price of the book all by itself.) In short, Kate and Nicole actually explain the things most of us had to absorb from context or learn by getting it wrong.

The second wonderful thing about the book is its unapologetic, matter-of-fact belief that humanness matters as much as formal expertise, and that compassion trumps cleverness. The result is a writing guide that grounds its wealth of practical advice in empathy for readers and their needs—and really digs into what that means, and how to go about understanding the culture, vocabulary, and sensibilities of the communities you write for.

Between them, Kate and Nicole have written for many of the web's most valuable and respected companies. Their commitment to clarity and kindness is the result of their experience, and it makes them extraordinary teachers. The sum of their efforts is an orderly, comprehensive method for accomplishing each writing project you undertake: not paint-by-numbers, but a flexible process within which you can focus all your attention on your goals, your readers, and their needs.

Good writing is always hard, but good guidance makes it a thousand times easier. I can't imagine better guides.

— Erin Kissane
 Author of *The Elements of Content Strategy*
 Director of Content, Knight-Mozilla OpenNews

STYLE MATTERS

YOU CAN'T SEE YOUR READERS. You don't know how they're feeling or what they're going through. You can't watch their expressions or make eye contact with them. So writing for them is a little bit of a puzzle.

Most companies fail at this. They don't know how to talk to people like real human beings, and their content is confusing or unhelpful. Sometimes it's even offensive. And that's a genuine problem, because there's no shortage of other things people can do or read online. You need readers to trust you.

With this book, our goal is to unravel the mysteries of the writing process and help you create useful and meaningful web content. Part of that is about asking the right questions. Part of it is about practicing and reading your work aloud. And part of it is about balancing your goals with what your readers need each step of the way.

Whether you're a writer, editor, blogger, content strategist, designer, developer, or small business owner, this book is for you. If you're new to the field, we'll introduce you to the types of content that go into making a website. If you're an experienced writer looking to brush up your skills, we'll help you take your voice further and thread your communications together.

In the chapters that follow, we'll show you how to write for the web with a consistent style and clear sense of purpose. You'll learn how to plan a writing project, define realistic goals, and work toward your mission. You'll know how to adapt your tone to fit the situation and match your readers' feelings. You'll have a set of principles to guide your writing. You'll be ready to teach these concepts to your team with a simple style guide. And you'll know when to break the rules.

This is not a handbook, a playbook, or a workbook. What follows is our best advice from years of writing for the web professionally. As you read, feel free to skip around to the parts that apply to what you're doing right now. After all, writing isn't a linear process. There's no real beginning, middle, or end.

We put a heavy emphasis on the fundamentals, ongoing practice, and value of writing. We won't go into detail about related disciplines like content strategy, information architecture, search engine optimization, or interaction design. But we included a list of our favorite resources in the Further Reading section.

Language is powerful. Your words can make people feel happy, sad, frustrated, proud, and everything in between. So whether or not "writer" is in your title, your writing is important. At the end of the day, you're a person communicating with other people. You want to be nice about it, and despite the screens between you and your readers, you *can* do that. That's why style matters. So let's get to it.

Happy writing!

Chapter One

WHAT WRITERS DO

DESPITE WHAT YOU MAY HAVE SEEN in the movies, you don't need a swanky office or a tweed jacket to be a writer. You don't even need a pair of dark-rimmed glasses (unless you do, of course).

You already communicate with people every day. You're nice to them. You build relationships with them. You encourage them and help them when they're confused. You persuade them to do things. You try to say the right thing at the right time. Those are the same skills it takes to be a web writer—and this book shows you how to bring them to the page.

This chapter introduces:

- The practice of web writing and why it matters
- The web writer's role
- Principles of good content
- How the writing process works

Let's start by looking at that word *content*. When we talk about copy or content, we're mostly talking about the text on your website. But in broader terms, you can think of content as anything you publish online or offline to help your readers and your business.

Web writing at work

You may write articles, blog posts, social media posts, product descriptions, marketing pages, help documents, legal contracts, and interface messages. You may write more general information about yourself too, like how to contact you and why you started your business. These are all pieces of web content. Emails and newsletters also fit into that definition, because people read them online and similar rules apply.

In the following chapters, we'll walk you through these different *content types*. We'll also cover a few things you write behind the scenes, like mission statements, project briefs, and style guides. These are important parts of your communications, and they can inform the rest of your writing.

Where writing comes in

Let's look at the situations where web writing matters and the challenges related to each one. We'll address these topics throughout the book.

Personal projects

If you have a portfolio or blog, you already know to put your heart and soul into your writing. Your readers expect your content to be a representation of you, your feelings, and your personal interests. Whether or not your website is a business, you probably have a few goals in mind. You may want to develop your voice as a writer or better understand your readers. With a personal site, it's useful to think about what you want to be known for. What story do you want to tell? To help with that, we'll show you how to extend your blog to a larger community, work with contributors, and promote yourself in a way that feels comfortable to you.

Small businesses

If you're running a small company, you already write different types of content every day. We'll help you do that in a more systematic way, so your communications are cohesive and manageable. Start by articulating

The Largest Wine Selection & Experts to Help You Choose

wine.com®

$30 OFF
Your Order of $100

Offer good through 10/31/16

Enter Code
SF30WINE

Free Shipping Options Available

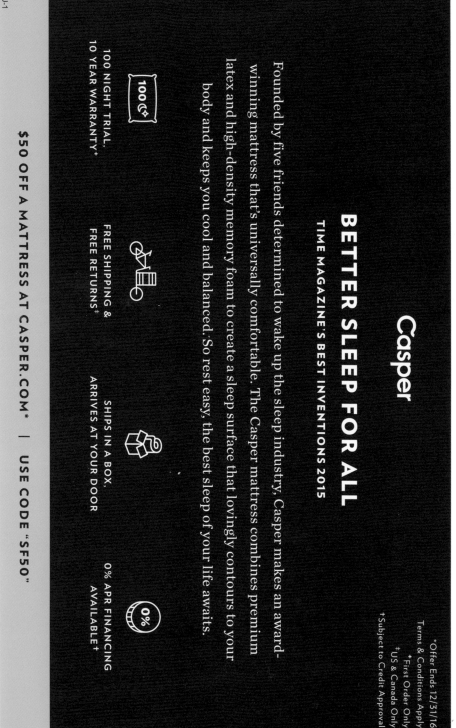

LOLA

100% organic cotton tampons • www.mylola.com

REAL WOMEN, REAL PRODUCTS

We care about the ingredients in our food and our face cream, but we'd never thought about what was in our tampons. LOLA tampons are made from 100% organic cotton with **no harsh chemicals, fragrances, or dyes.**

WHY SUBSCRIBE?

It's time to ditch the drugstore: get exactly what you need, exactly when you need it. Pick your perfect mix, number of boxes, and how often you need them and we'll deliver directly to your door.

Shipping is always free.

Get 60% off your first order with code SF60

This too shall pass

and until it does, we're here for you!

. . . .

www.mylola.com

This box contains your
customized assortment of eighteen
100% cotton tampons.

LOLA tampons are unscented
and enclosed in compact
plastic applicators for your
convenience.

LOLA tampons contain no additives,
synthetics, chemicals or dyes.
Our product is made in-house
and packaged in the US.

Questions?
hello@mylola.com

LOLA

SF-AU-4B

LOLA

www.mylola.com

100% organic cotton tampons | Delivered to your door

your goals and your mission. Keep those things in mind as you improve your website for your customers and grow your business over time.

Freelancing

As a consultant or independent contractor, you probably switch between writing, editing, and making recommendations to clients. You have to manage the entire process, from doing quick research to summarizing a project plan, and getting through the writing itself. We'll share tips for taking in feedback and getting unstuck, which is especially important when you're working remotely or by yourself.

Agencies

If you write for an agency, you may do a mix of copywriting for clients and writing for the studio itself. In client services, you have to manage several different projects and relationships at the same time. You probably have a design team, a project manager, and a strategy team to support you. You'll learn how to write more collaboratively and organize your recommendations into clear deliverables for your clients.

Startups

If you're at a scrappy new company, you may be scrambling to figure out what's important to focus on. We'll show how to keep your writing purposeful, promote your latest products, and think about communication as a larger process. We'll also teach you how to write copy for apps and web interfaces with a style that suits your growing company.

Companies and nonprofits

At an established organization, you may not have the flexibility to change how things are done. A big part of your job is figuring out how to write well in the existing organizational structure. You'll want to focus on copy that directly affects the bottom line. You may have a chance to update your brand or writing style, especially if it's out of date. We'll show you how to talk to different audiences and teach these concepts to other writers so you can keep a consistent voice.

Your role may change, and there may be some overlap, but we all share similar content principles.

Content principles

Good content is clear, useful, and friendly. It helps you work toward your goals and speaks directly to your readers. We'll go over each of these principles one by one, and come back to them throughout the book.

Clear

The web is riddled with confusing prose and mixed messages. One way to stand out is to work hard on every single sentence. Watch out for fuzzy concepts, jargon, and unfinished thoughts. Understand your topic and talk about it in as few words as possible. That can take a long time. As William Zinsser says, "A clear sentence is no accident."[1] But it's worth it. You're writing for people with limited time and attention, and you may be short on space. Be sure your writing makes sense and gets the point across quickly.

Useful

Everything you publish should serve a purpose. As you work on a piece, ask yourself: How does it support your goals? How does it align with your mission? Does it teach people something new? Choose topics your readers care about; don't worry about what everyone else is doing. Think about how to convey the information, too: Would it make an interesting blog post? Or would it be better in your help center? When and where you share information can be as important as the words you use.

Friendly

Few companies take the time to be nice in their writing. But if you're like us, you want readers to know that you genuinely care about them and that you're listening. Your content is the perfect place to do this. There are many ways to be friendly: by choosing precise words, finding the

---

1 William Zinsser, *On Writing Well*, 7th ed. (New York: Collins, 2006), 9.

right tone, and developing a relatable writing style. A warm, clear voice can help readers find what they need and relieve stressful situations. Friendly content keeps people coming back, and might even make them smile.

What it takes

When you're faced with a new writing project, it can be tempting to open a blank document and start typing away. But it's not always the best idea to dive in headfirst. Take some time to think about where you're going and how you'll get there. Writing good content is hard work—and not all of it happens on the page or on the screen. Here are some good habits to practice:

Be curious and patient with yourself. This will help you think long and hard about language and topics, so you can convey your ideas in the kindest and clearest way possible.

Remember that you're writing for real people. They have feelings, needs, and busy lives. In a way, the web is a customer service medium.[2] Your customers may not always be right, but they always deserve your thoughtfulness and respect. Unless you want to sound like a robot, you have to be conversational—and sometimes even a little touchy-feely—in your writing.

Listen hard. Pay attention to feedback from your colleagues and your community. That will keep you grounded as your readership grows. Many companies talk about themselves for themselves by themselves, with little concern for anyone else. That isn't helpful. Think about how your readers want to hear from you, and talk to them at a human level. Find a way to write that sounds like you *and* appeals to your audience. You don't have to be all business all the time, and you don't need to seem infallible.

Get comfortable selling yourself. Marketing can feel gross, because— let's face it—a lot of it is gross. But people are busy and there are a

---

2 Paul Ford, "The Web Is a Customer Service Medium," Ftrain, January 6, 2011, www.ftrain.com/wwic.html

million other websites to look at. So if you're selling something online, you need to make yourself or your company stand out. You need to tell people what you're doing, but you *don't* have to fake it—and nobody wants you to. If you're genuinely excited, that will shine through in your writing.

Approaching your content in a thoughtful and open-minded way will help make it clear, friendly, and useful. Now, let's look at an overview of the writing process.

The process

Every project is different, and every team is too. Your process will depend on several factors: what you're writing about, who you're writing for, and how you work best. Most writing projects include four repeatable steps (**Figure 1.1**).

RESEARCH   CLARIFY   WRITE   REFINE

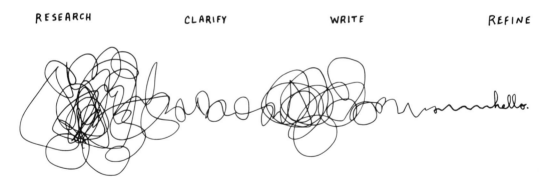

FIGURE 1.1 The writing process is messy. You may need to revisit steps along the way.

Step 1: Research

It's impossible to be clear, useful, *or* friendly if you don't know what you're talking about. So start with solid research. Figure out what your readers need and what they expect from you. Define your short-term and long-term goals. Speed up the writing process by taking notes and organizing your thoughts. (We'll show you how to do that in Chapter 2: Get Your Bearings.)

Step 2: Clarify

Once you get your head around the project, clarify your goals and make a plan with your team. Summarize your decisions, along with any informal conversations you've had. Establish why this project matters, what you're going to write, and what you want your content to do. Set a timeframe for achieving these goals, even if it changes later. (We'll talk about that in Chapter 3: Make a Plan.)

Step 3: Write

After you figure out what you want to say, it's time to sit down and write. Try a few copy variations to see what works best. Play with the words and phrases. Then, revise the draft until it's ready to publish. Check for typos, inconsistencies, and repetitive ideas. Cut anything that's not useful for readers. If you can, show early drafts to friends or coworkers. (We'll share exercises throughout the book to help you with this step.)

Step 4: Refine

Once you finalize a draft (yay! hooray!), it's time to publish it—but that doesn't mean your work is finished. Keep your content current and improve it over time. Listen for feedback from friends, customers, and coworkers. Would templates, checklists, or style guidelines help you the next time around?

Writing is a fluid process. You may need to update existing copy, remove outdated information, or add new pages down the line. The web makes it easy to revise your work, so take advantage of that.

Meet Shortstack Books

There are plenty of good and bad writing examples out there—and we'll share some with you. But to keep our own writing clear, useful, and friendly, we'll use an imaginary children's bookstore (**Figure 1.2**) as a running example throughout this book. (It's not a real place, but we wish it were!)

FIGURE 1.2 The storefront of our imaginary bookstore.

Shortstack Books carries new and collectible titles, and the owners want to try selling some of them online. Shortstack will need to bridge the gap between the retail store and the online shop. This presents a few challenges.

First, how will people find the new shop? Shortstack could tell regular customers that they're launching a web shop, but they'll want to tell people in other cities too. Blog posts and newsletters could help them get the word out.

Second, how will Shortstack describe the condition of their used books to online shoppers who can't flip through them? Including photos, descriptions, and notes about each title, like whether or not it was signed, would help. These are good selling points.

Third, what will make people buy directly from Shortstack's website instead of someplace else? It will be important to highlight what's special about the shop. Friendly interface copy would also improve the shopping experience.

These are all problems that good writing can solve: promoting something, telling people what it's all about, and guiding them through a process. We'll work toward these goals as we build up the shop.

Chapter Two

GET YOUR BEARINGS

THINK ABOUT THE LAST TIME you made something from scratch. Maybe you cook dinner on weeknights, or you enjoy making furniture by hand. Whenever you're planning a project, you probably think about what you want to make, who it's for, what it needs to do, and how to pull it all together. That kind of thinking is problem solving, and we all do it every day. But most people don't approach writing this way—and that makes it harder than it needs to be.

Whether you're making a meal, a table, or a website, you need to think about your goals and your audiences. In this chapter, you'll learn how to:

- Do high-level research to get a sense of history
- Conduct interviews with colleagues, clients, and readers
- Understand your audiences and cover meaningful topics for them
- Write a mission statement

These exercises will help you get your bearings so that you can balance what readers need to know with what you want to tell them.

Do your research

Good writing doesn't happen on its own. It takes its sweet time, and it needs a reason for being. From the outside, the process may sound simple enough: do some research, think about what you want to say, write it down, clean it up, and put it out there. But as everyone knows, it can be tricky to put something meaningful into words—especially if you're not sure who's going to read it. Writers aren't magicians. The term *wordsmith* reminds us of that; smiths are craftspeople who forge raw materials into useful shapes.

As a writer, your initial research should help you:

- Understand the material
- Define your goals and mission (purpose)
- Connect with readers and address their needs (audiences)
- Decide how you want to talk to readers (style)

It may take several rounds of interviews and conversations to narrow down those decisions, especially in the early stages.

Study up

Start by getting acquainted with your material. Take notes. Immerse yourself in it. You may need to read up on specific topics or interview people on your team to understand their needs. If you're writing about something you love, think about why it matters to you and how it helps other people. If you're writing about a product or a feature, start by talking to the experts on your team. Figure out what readers need to know.

You can also look at how other companies explain similar topics. See what language they use, and how they connect the dots for readers. Is there anything that makes your company different? As you read, think about what works and what doesn't. Find a way to make your material relatable and interesting for your readers. A quick comparison study can help you with that.

Set clear goals

The most important thing you can do to strengthen your writing is to define clear goals. Focus on why the topic matters for you and your different audiences. What do people actually need? Work toward that.

If you're not sure why people come to your website, follow that question. Decide which actions you want readers to take on your website too. Maybe you want to help them learn something new or feel more confident in their decisions. When you know what people need and what you want them to do, you can prioritize those topics and skip anything that isn't worth your time. After all, your writing should be practical for your business and your readers. Make a habit of thinking about your goals *and* your readers' goals each time you sit down to write.

For many writers, research is the fun part. You can learn new things, think about long-term goals, and even meet some of your readers. But it doesn't have to slow you down. In most cases, research speeds up the writing process, because it gives you a foundation to work from and helps you organize your thoughts. You don't need six months of user studies or a comprehensive plan to start writing, but you should have a tiny pinhole of an idea of what you're trying to do.

Keep looking forward, asking questions, and reflecting on where you want to take people. We'll start that process here and continue it throughout the book.

Conduct interviews

Before you start writing, take some time to learn about your readers, your colleagues, and your clients. Whether you're at a new job or on a new project, interviews are a great way to understand what's important right now.

Make new friends

Good writing doesn't happen in isolation. Your words are there to inform readers, guide them, and help them get on with their day. Interviews help you grasp what readers are trying to do and make that happen.

Start by interviewing people you'll be working with regularly. You could meet with members of your design team, your project manager, or your main client contacts. Choose people who understand your audiences and the material you're writing about. You may even want to interview directors or your CEO, depending on the size of your company. If you work for yourself, talk to a few friends or customers over coffee to make sure your plans address their needs.

No matter who you're interviewing, the point of having these conversations is to understand other people's needs and address them in your writing. Here are a few other reasons to come out from behind your desk and talk to people:

Gather consensus. Regular check-ins and interviews will keep your writing in sync with your team and your clients. By gathering up people's goals and opinions, you're not only making them feel included in the process, but also taking in their feedback before you even sit down to write.

Choose clear, friendly language. If your company is talking about something in one way and your readers talk about it in another way, you'll notice those differences in your conversations and be able to correct them. Interviews can improve the overall quality of your writing by keeping it accurate, honest, and relevant.

Improve your process. On a new project, interviews can help you understand how your content will move through the publishing process. You'll learn who's in charge of each step, who will approve your drafts, and how best to share them.

Internal interviews with Pinterest's Tiffani Jones Brown

Tiffani Jones Brown is the writing team manager at Pinterest in San Francisco. When she joined Pinterest, her goal was to build a team of writers to be the voice of the company. But first, she had to figure out what that voice really was. She began with what she calls organizational anthropological work—by interviewing Pinterest's founders, community manager, designers, researchers, and engineers. She asked questions like:

> How would you describe Pinterest?
>
> Tell me the story of Pinterest. How did we get to where we are?
>
> Why do you like working here? What makes this place feel special?
>
> When you look at our logo, what adjectives come to mind?

These conversations helped Tiffani understand how different people on her team think about the company. She says, "The way that I work best is to figure out what the landscape is and then try to boil those things down into basic concepts. I build up a pile of notes and pick out the parts that feel poignant and consistent from everyone." Research and listening are the foundation of Tiffani's writing process. She took what she learned in these interviews to start developing Pinterest's voice and tone guidelines. Her findings also helped her understand how the writing team fits into Pinterest as a whole.

She wants to see things from an outside perspective, so she thinks like an executive. "I have to be choosy about what I get worked up about. I try to be really respectful of people and learn how to work within the organizational structure," she says. If there's a disagreement, she tries to resolve it by listening, asking questions, and making sure everyone understands one another—or backing off when it's not an important time for her team to be involved. Having a sense of history helps Tiffani keep a perspective and focus on long-term goals. She says: "If you're a good communicator, everything comes from that: the words, the design, and the process. It's all about figuring out how to communicate best."

Find the expert. During your research, you may find that it would be better for a subject-matter expert to take a shot at a draft, instead of having you try to learn everything about the topic. In that scenario, you'll take on the role of editor and help the contributing writer touch on important points while staying true to your style so readers can relate.

Interview tips

Let's go over general tips for running effective interviews.

Be prepared

Think about what you want to learn ahead of time. Is this a working session or do you need a lot of information from the other person? What's the best format for the conversation? It's helpful to see facial expressions, but there will be times when you need to interview someone over the phone or by email. Pick a format for the interview that will help you get the best answers. If you plan to record it, test out your equipment beforehand and ask for permission ahead of time.

Start with broad topics

Write down a few questions and order them so they flow like a natural conversation. Your goal is to understand the other person's needs and perspective so that you can keep those things in mind as you write. Start with broad questions. Here are some examples:

- What are you trying to accomplish?
- How can the content support you and your goals?
- Are you having any problems with the website? Or are there any changes you'd like to see?
- What's working right now? What isn't working?

Try to make each question neutral and open. Rewrite anything that leans in a specific direction or lends itself to a simple yes or no response. Give the person you're interviewing a chance to surprise you.

Keep it conversational

As you move through each question, let the other person reflect on the topic and give you a full answer. Leave room for awkward silences. You can chime in occasionally to build on their ideas, but resist the urge to interrupt or finish their sentences. A good interview feels more like a conversation than a Q&A. Be prepared to deviate from your question list. The most important thing is to show the other person that you're listening.

Keep it short

Plan to chat for about 30–45 minutes. If you think you'll need more time, break the interview into two sessions so you can absorb everything that's been said. You'll need to do research and interviews throughout the writing process, so don't try to cram it all in. Mary Pipher, author of *Writing to Change the World*, says interviewing is not a linear process for her:

> Starting out, I often conduct some interviews to determine the lay of the land, then, later, other interviews to understand nuances or fill in gaps. Toward the end of a project, I often have more sophisticated and focused questions to explore, so I will schedule a few last-minute interviews to get answers.[1]

You can follow up afterwards, in person or with an email.

Say what happens next

After thanking the person for their time, let them know what happens next. Are you gathering background information or almost ready to share a draft? Or are you interviewing other readers before updating your website? Give the interviewee a sense of what you're working on and let them ask you questions too. Make time for their questions at the beginning and the end of the interview.

---

1 Mary Pipher, *Writing to Change the World* (New York: Riverhead, 2006), 129.

User interviews with Jodi Leo

Jodi Leo is the head of product and design at Imprint, and previously served as the director of UX at Bolt | Peters. She shared these wonderful tips for understanding readers—whether you're conducting interviews, posting a survey, or having a casual conversation behind the scenes. "When most people try to get the bottom of real behaviors and motivations, they start to get into the imaginary zone," she says. "If you don't base the design on talking to real humans, you run the risk of creating fluff—and fluff attracts fluff." To keep her work grounded in reality, Jodi talks to her users and updates the website based on their feedback. Here's how she approaches those conversations:

Think it through. Consider the most important aspects of your products and services. What are the main parts or features? What do they mean to your readers? Jodi says most people skip this step before doing interviews, but it's important to know what you want to learn in advance.

See where they are on different spectrums. Find out how readers interact with the kinds of information you offer. For example, for a food publication, you may want to map out these spectrums:

> How do readers think and feel about food?
>
> What do they want and need from food sites?
>
> How do they interact with recipes and other food writing?
>
> What is their goal? Are they researching, planning an event, or reading for pleasure?

See where you fit in, and keep that in mind as you write.

Get them to tell you stories. Ask people how they found you, but phrase the question carefully. Don't ask, "Would you search for 'meaningful gift' on Google?" Make it more neutral, like: "How would you define a keepsake?" or "When was the last time you gave someone a meaningful gift?" Try to get people to tell you stories about themselves. You may learn something and even inspire your readers by asking. As Jodi says: "People are often just enchanted that you care to hear about their adventures with the internet."

Know your readers

If you can interview your readers, you'll have a strong sense of their needs. But if you can't talk to them, you'll have to make some educated guesses. Let's work through a few exercises to help you with that.

Define your audiences

Your readers are the main reason you're here. But *who* are they exactly? If you're working with clients or colleagues, take some time to talk about your different audiences and define who you're trying to reach.

Think about your goals and how your company relates to the community around you. Who's going to use your website regularly? For Shortstack Books, the most obvious answer would be: anyone who would buy a children's book online. But let's go further than that. We can choose several audiences to focus on, and put them into primary and secondary categories. Here's one take on that:

> Primary audiences: kids and their parents
>
> Secondary audiences: grandparents, teachers, and people who collect children's books

We could refine this list with more detailed attributes too. Maybe we want to focus on families within a specific city or state, or kids up to 12 years of age.

Think about the attributes and demographics your readers have in common. Consider their education level, geographic area, and economic situation. Are they mostly tech savvy, or do they have differing levels of familiarity with the web? Look into the devices and websites they use regularly. Ask yourself how familiar they are with the topics you're covering.

Whenever you make assumptions about your readers, check them against your goals and real-world experience. Consider how different people use different parts of your website. For example, with Shortstack Books, the checkout flow may be there to help adults complete a

purchase, but the homepage and book descriptions could be fun
and appealing to kids, too. Remember that different people have
different needs and feelings—and those things change depending on
the situation. The point of thinking about your audiences and their
commonalities (or differences) is to help you picture them and keep these
things in mind as you write.

Write to people you know

Next time you're planning a big project, try making a list of topics you
want to cover based on people you know in real life. Here's how we did
that for this book. This exercise took about two hours—and if you're like
us, you'll want to have markers, sticky notes, and snacks nearby.

Make a list of takeaways

We began by asking ourselves why the book matters and what we want
people to learn from it. We wrote each topic that came to mind on its
own blue sticky note until we ran out of ideas. Then, we grouped the
related topics together. Those groups became the chapters. We wrote
tentative chapter titles on yellow sticky notes and put those beside
each group.

Remember your audiences

Next, we talked about different kinds of people who write for the web.
We thought about what they have in common and how their needs differ
from one another. We narrowed it down to six roles: writers, editors,
bloggers, small business owners, developers, and designers. Then, we
wrote those roles on red sticky notes.

Name a few representatives

For the last step, we chose a representative for each of the red
sticky notes. We picked someone we know in real life who has that
role, and wrote down their name and title like this: "Vivian, small
business owner."

Then, we went through the chapters one by one, and talked about topics we wanted to cover for each person, such as:

> What does Vivian need from this chapter?
> How can voice and tone help Lesley with her writing?
> What will give Jon the confidence to write this on his own?

As we filled in the outline with topics, we checked each chapter to make sure it addressed each person's needs and expectations for their role. When we finished, we had a detailed outline organized into chapters. This helped us start writing and tie everything together. You can do this same exercise for a larger set of pages or articles to keep your writing focused on what people actually need.

Write a mission statement

Now that you have a better sense of what you're doing and who you're writing for, let's talk about your biggest goal: your mission.

Your mission is your purpose—the reason behind your work. It could be a lofty idea, like why you started your company, or why you keep it going. It could be more practical and talk about the purpose of your blog, of your team, or of a particular project. A meaningful mission statement helps you ground your work and share your values with other people.

If you're on a team, you may need to write collaboratively, and that creates challenges for everyone involved. When several people contribute to the same website, you run the risk of contradicting one another or talking about things in slightly different ways. But if everyone is working toward your mission with clear priorities and style guidelines, your writing will naturally reflect that clarity.

A mission statement can guide your writing in the same ways that a business plan guides product decisions. You can look back on it and keep things on track over a longer period of time. Depending on what you do, you may call this a brand strategy or purpose statement. It's not a tagline or marketing message, but we'll cover those later in the book. And we're not talking about those vague, monotonous mission statements you see on corporate websites. You know the ones: *We are industry leaders, dedicated to improving our customers' lives. Our company provides a range of innovative solutions for businesses at all stages. Integrity, success, and value. Blah blah blah.*

Real-world examples

Let's look at some examples from popular brands. As you read through each one, consider what you like and don't like. Notice any words or images that stand out. Do these ideas line up with how you perceive the companies?

New York magazine:

> Simultaneously enthusiastic and skeptical, *New York* magazine is obsessively concerned with the new, the undiscovered, the next. New York connects engaged readers with original ideas, and customers with brands, products, and services that help them live well and become the most active and influential participants in the cultural conversation.

Chronicle Books:

> Inspired by the enduring magic and importance of books, our objective is to create and distribute exceptional publishing that's instantly recognizable for its spirit, creativity, and value. This objective also informs our business relationships and endeavors, be they with customers, authors, vendors, or colleagues.

charity: water:

> charity: water is a non-profit organization bringing clean and safe drinking water to people in developing nations.

Starbucks:

> Our mission: to inspire and nurture the human spirit—one person, one cup and one neighborhood at a time.

TED:

> Our mission: Spread ideas

Google:

> Google's mission is to organize the world's information and make it universally accessible and useful.

These statements work on different levels. TED's is mostly inspirational, while Google's is more straightforward. charity: water's is practical and specific. The Starbucks corporate mission to "inspire and nurture the human spirit" wouldn't communicate a clear image, if it weren't for that "one cup at a time" (read: coffee) at the end. *New York* magazine's statement captures the spirit of New York City. And Chronicle Books uses an especially memorable word: magic.

Who, what, and why

A good mission statement is both practical and aspirational. Answer questions like these:

- What makes us different?
- What do we do, and why does it matter?
- What problems are we solving?
- What's our philosophy?
- If we're successful, what will be different in 5–10 years?

Think about how you want to express your mission and bring it to life. Start by writing down answers to these questions. Then, combine the words into a cohesive sentence or paragraph and whittle down the text. One by one, remove unimportant words and statements that aren't exactly true. Pare it down to a few short sentences. Every word has to work hard here, so consider each one carefully and make sure the language accurately describes your brand or project. Don't overpromise. Your mission statement should be inspiring and honest to set the tone for your other communications.

Mission statement Mad Libs

If you need help, try an exercise like the Mad Libs games. Write some basic sentence structures that could work for you. It's okay if they're dry right now; don't worry about the exact wording yet. Here are a few places to start:

We make (plural noun) for (audience noun).

We help (audience noun) (verb) (adverb).

We want to (verb) (noun) to (verb) so they can (verb) (adverb).

Next, fill in the blanks with words and phrases that work for you. You can do this exercise with a whiteboard, or with notecards on a big table. Treat each word as a variable that can change.

Let's work through an example for Shortstack Books. Here are some ideas for audience nouns:

readers

kids

children

people

customers

Which of these feel right? Since Shortstack is primarily for kids, the first three seem like the best fit for now. Let's go with the "We want to…" phrasing to start. You could say:

We want to inspire children to read so they can live curiously.

Not too bad. This version calls out what we want to accomplish and why. It gives you the gist. You could add more personality or details, like regions or age groups:

We want to inspire children of all ages to read so they can live healthy, curious lives.

That's a little warmer at the beginning, but then drops off a bit. Start with something simple to get the conversation going. Once you find a direction, work on refining it. Let's cut out the inessential elements and add one or two concrete examples:

> We want to help children discover the joys of reading and living curiously. Everything we offer—from our hand-picked selection of books to our weekly events and summer reading camps—brings us closer to that mission.

That's more like it. It doesn't have to be perfect, but it should align with your values and sound like you. When you're finished, you should have something you'd be proud to print out and tape up by your desk.

Some companies put their mission statements on their websites, but we recommend thinking of it as an internal tool. Turning it into a marketing message can dilute its meaning for your employees, and they're the people it's supposed to benefit most. It can also spark cynicism in your customers if your service doesn't live up to it. Whether you share your mission statement publicly or keep it to yourself, use it as a compass for your writing as you go forward.

Keep the balance

When you're planning a project and deciding what to prioritize—or how to approach a specific message—weigh that against your mission and your readers' needs. Work toward a balance.

In some cases, you may need to dig into lower-level project goals before talking about your mission, voice, and tone. Even if you're still figuring things out, you can start writing now. Communication is an ongoing process, so keep that in mind and revisit your goals regularly.

Chapter Three

MAKE A PLAN

Now that you understand your goals and audiences, it's time to plan out the project. Depending on what you're doing, a writing project can have many moving parts. If you work on a creative team or with clients, this chapter will help you collaborate with them, talk through your goals, and plan your content. If you work for yourself or as a freelancer, it will help you write practical project briefs and sketch out your writing in chunks, to create a framework for what's ahead. You'll learn how to:

- Clarify and summarize your project goals
- Get everyone on the same page before you start writing
- Write a project brief or communication plan
- Pick content types to help your readers
- Approach writing in a modular way

These skills will help you keep your projects running smoothly and get ready to write web copy.

Clarify your goals

Goals mean different things to different people. You may have specific goals, like wanting to sell 10,000 units of a product in a month, or increase your readership by 10 percent, or raise $250,000 in donations by the end of the quarter. You may have squishy goals, like raising awareness about your brand or working against misconceptions people have about you. Your readers have goals too.

Start every project the same way: Do your research, and then clarify what you want to accomplish and how your content can advance that goal. Maybe you need a style guide in the next few weeks, or you want to establish an editorial process to support publishing new essays each month. Maybe you're redesigning an entire website or launching a newsletter. These are all goals that a writer can help with.

It takes many different skills and personality types to run a successful business or website. There may be some natural tension on your team or between you and your clients. For example, at a large company, engineering is often focused on moving faster and more efficiently, while writers need time to reflect and consider every piece of copy that goes out. That kind of contrast is a positive thing—it means that everyone is doing their job. But it's important to investigate those situations before you start writing so you know how to proceed.

Write a goal statement

Once you have a goal in mind, make it concrete by putting it into words. Goal statements are helpful for any writer, and they can rally your team around the cause. Even if you're working alone, writing a goal statement is a good way to get your head around a project. Here are some tips for doing that:

Be specific. Say what will change if your website or project does its job. Your goal has to mean something for the people working on it, so make it concrete and easy to understand. If you need to say more, explain why this goal matters for your business and your readers. Include a deadline or time frame.

Be practical. Choose goals you can achieve with your team. Make sure everyone is comfortable with the plan too. If your goal is unrealistic, you won't achieve it, and that defeats the purpose of writing it in the first place. A goal is there to help you stay motivated and make gradual progress together.

Add metrics. Include dollar amounts, numbers of customers, or data points when you can. Metrics help you track and measure your content over time.

A strong goal statement says what you're doing and helps you see what you're *not* doing. Here are some examples:

> In the next six months, we want to raise donations by 30%.

> In the next six weeks, we want to increase new subscriptions from this button by 5%.

> In the next 12 months, we want to make this site the best resource for our developer community.

> After launching the web shop, we want to sell $2,500 worth of books in the first two weeks.

Keep it concise, but don't cut any important details. You may have multiple goals, so write as many statements as you need.

Kickoff meetings with Corey Vilhauer

Corey Vilhauer is a user experience strategist at Blend Interactive, a design and development agency in Sioux Falls. Corey's role is a mix of writing, content strategy, and information architecture. As a consultant, he sees his role as a facilitator. He's not always doing all the writing, but he wants to help clients persevere. Since his work touches on writing, branding, design, and project planning, he likes to start each project with a kickoff meeting.

Corey invites the entire client team to sit down together to discuss their goals and audiences. Having everyone in the room from the beginning keeps them on the same page and helps them work out a realistic project plan. "We call our discovery process a workshop, because we're asking our clients to do the work," he says. "We're there to capture the thoughts they're having and help them structure a process for developing the content." He likes to include everyone who's involved in the publishing process: writers, designers, marketing managers, store managers, and even the CEO.

After his clients agree on their goals, Corey figures out what kinds of skills they have, how they're making content now, and which parts of the process they enjoy most. Next, they work out a plan for accomplishing their goals. That could include hiring more writers, changing their publishing process, or even adjusting which content types they publish regularly. Those kinds of changes can be stressful—and even redefine someone's role at the company—so he makes a point to be empathetic and encouraging. He uses terminology that his clients are comfortable with. "We've made a big effort to take the stuff we talk about in meetings and discovery workshops and make it relatable to words they're using within their company or within their workflow," he says. "It's about working with people to create more of a partnership, and more of a system where there can be feedback." Talking about content and website goals as a team can help you get there.

Summarize the plan

You may want to summarize your goals and audience needs in a detailed document rather than a short list of goal statements. These sorts of documents have different names—proposals, creative briefs, communication plans, research summaries, and discovery documents— but they all have a similar purpose: to summarize what you know about a project. To keep it simple, we'll call them *project briefs*. Feel free to adapt this format and call it whatever makes sense for you.

A project brief outlines your goals and your plans for achieving them. You could use this document to help your team prepare for a website redesign, or to elaborate on why you're launching a blog. You could also use it to summarize your content research for a client, share editorial recommendations with your team, or pitch the next phase of a copywriting project. Many clients expect you to give them a brief before you start writing.

A good project brief clarifies what the project is, why it matters, who will benefit from it, what the goals are, and who's involved. It can also include notes about things that could slow down the plan, like needing to hire someone or update the website to accommodate new content types. Cover the most important points for your internal audience. And like it says in the name, it should be *brief* so it's easy to digest.

The purpose of this multipart (but not always multipage) document is to get everyone up to speed on the project or convince them it's worth doing. It may make sense to write it collaboratively with your team, especially in an agency environment. You could have each member of your team write a section or chat about the plan together and then have one person write the whole thing.

Write a project brief

The format is a simple outline, which forces you to organize your thoughts so people can follow along. Pick and choose the parts that apply to you.

Project summary

Introduce the project in a few sentences. Frame up the most important points, including what you're trying to do, why it matters, and where you want to be afterward. Sell it if you need to. Draw attention to any decisions that need to be made, either with a list of next steps or open questions. If the project is already in progress, summarize what you've learned so far, or highlight your recommendations for what to do next.

Goals

List each of your goal statements here. You may need separate sections for business, website, and content goals. Remember to be realistic and include metrics if you have them.

Audiences

Summarize what you know about your readers. What are they trying to do? What do they need? Be specific about their interests and demographics. Say how your writing can support their priorities. A project brief for Shortstack Books might say that the site should be friendly for parents, teachers, kids, and grandparents—and those readers will sometimes have different needs. If you're writing for international audiences, you could also highlight special considerations for translations.

Content types

List the different content types related to this project, like blog posts, marketing copy, product descriptions, or help documents. Include details about the length and purpose of each one. If you need images or other design assets for any of the content types, call those out. (We'll talk about content types in more detail later in this chapter.)

Sample topics

List specific topics that you'll cover regularly. These should tie back to your goals and mission. The list doesn't have to be comprehensive, but it should help your team understand what you're planning to write. For example, the Shortstack website could feature new arrivals on the blog and send email newsletters about seasonal sales, reading camps, and upcoming events. We could go further too with general topics about reading, parenting, and the history of children's books.

Marketing messages

Add details about why your product, service, or website matters. Your writing should convey these messages without necessarily stating them word for word. Narrow it down to a handful of points. If you looked at competitors' or inspiration sites, you could also include points for differentiation here. (See Chapter 8: Sell It Without Selling Out for more about marketing messages.)

Style notes

If you want to call attention to your style guide or make specific style recommendations for the project, add those notes here. In a blog plan, for example, you might tell contributors that their writing should be less formal than the help content and that they should use sentence case for titles, if that's your style.

Technical considerations

If anything needs to be built or changed at a system level to support your plan, like website development or a new content management system, include those technical considerations. You could also talk about how the text will be formatted, any chosen limitations, or broader workflow topics.

Project plan

Outline the work plan. How will your team accomplish these goals together? Include details about next steps, deadlines, and milestones. Specify how you'll develop the content with the time and resources you have now. On a large project, you could name members of the team and outline their responsibilities. Build in time for draft reviews and production or design work, if necessary. If any of the milestones could shift, mention that here. Show people where they are in the process so they know what's coming next.

Sample project brief

Let's look at an example for Shortstack's new online shop:

Shortstack Books: Shop launch

Summary

Shortstack is ready to start selling new and rare children's books to the good people of the internet. We want to build a web shop and launch it by October 1. Our plan is to start with a simple shop and add more personality and products as we grow online sales.

Goals

- Leading up to the launch, we want to drum up excitement about the new website and tell in-store customers to refer their friends.

- After launching the web shop, we want to sell $2,500 worth of books in the first two weeks.

- In the first six months, we want to increase our overall sales of rare and collectible books by 15%.

Audiences

- Primary: kids and their parents

- Secondary: teachers, grandparents, and children's book collectors

We want to produce clear, friendly copy that makes it easy for customers to find great books and get through checkout quickly.

Content types

Marketing copy; book descriptions; event descriptions; blog posts; email newsletters; contact info; About page; interface copy in the shop; shipping and sales policies; support info; occasional Twitter updates

Sample blog and newsletter topics

New arrivals; in-store exclusives; upcoming in-store events; summer reading camps; seasonal sales; interesting articles about reading, literacy, and children's books

Marketing messages

- Primary: We handpick every book so you don't have to.

- Secondary: We've been in business for 10 years. You can trust us to carry the best books in excellent condition.

Technical considerations

We want to integrate the website with Shopify and keep our voice consistent from one step to the next.

That's a good start. This summary will help you get going on the copy, and could also help a designer or developer understand what you're trying to achieve on the website.

Whenever you're writing a project brief, ask your team to give you feedback on it before you wrap it up. Most of the time, this sort of internal document helps everyone get their thoughts together at the outset of a project. But if you plan to use it as a guide or ongoing reference, update it as things change.

Dive in

Once you're clear on your goals and everyone's on the same page, it's time to plan the writing itself. For the rest of this chapter, we'll talk about the drafting process, which includes choosing content types, putting them into an outline, and creating a rough draft. Let's start by picking the right content types for your project.

Pick content types

Some projects will be limited to one content type, like blog posts or marketing copy, and others will include a variety of them. Each content type has a different purpose and format. What you publish will depend on your business, your readers, and your goals.

Here's a list to help you think about the different kinds of copy (**Table 3.1**). We'll cover most of these in the coming chapters.

TABLE 3.1 Content types for web writers

Editorial copy	Articles, blog posts, research studies
Marketing copy	Marketing pages, email newsletters, bios, product and event descriptions, promotions, case studies and customer stories, press releases, white papers, social media posts, ads
Interface copy	Buttons, links, navigation labels, product tours, instructions, tooltips, confirmation messages (subscribe, unsubscribe, saved changes), alerts, error messages, transactional emails (order confirmations, receipts, invoices), flows, forms, app notifications
User-generated content	Comments, ratings, reviews, stories, testimonials
Support content	Contact forms, email and chat canned responses, help center articles, guides and how-tos, technical documentation, FAQs, compliance alerts, downtime notifications
Policies and legal contracts	Terms of service, privacy policies, disclosures, partner and vendor agreements, community guidelines, account shutdown messages
Internal communications	Emails and memos, employee guidelines, handbooks and training, pitches and proposals, project briefs, style guides, brand assets

Let's figure out what makes sense for Shortstack. For the shop launch, we want people to buy books and sign up for events, so we'll need to feature those items on the website. Descriptions for books and events will help us do that. We could promote the shop with blog posts, an email newsletter, and general marketing copy, like shipping and holiday promotions. We could also post occasional Twitter updates, because some customers love hearing about in-store specials and upcoming events there, too.

To introduce the shop to new customers, we could have a short About page and put our contact info in the footer. And since this is a web shop, we'll need interface copy on the store pages, along with shipping policies, sales policies, and support info. That should cover it for now.

Here's a quick summary of those content types:

Marketing copy

Featured books in the shop (book descriptions)

Featured events (event descriptions)

Sales and promotional copy

Newsletter callout and signup form

Blog posts and social media posts

Interface copy

Checkout forms and field names

Confirmation and error messages

Links to the About, Blog, and Shop pages (navigation)

Support, policies, and general info

Contact info

About page copy

Support info

Sales and shipping policies

Now, let's turn that list into a rough outline.

Organize your thoughts

You can't write everything at once, so pick a representative page or content type to start with. Pull your notes together. Then, make an outline for yourself. Think of it as a glorified checklist to help you organize your thoughts and structure the piece.

On a small scale, you could outline a specific article or piece of copy. On a larger scale, you might make an outline for a homepage, a marketing page, or even your entire website. Start by listing the individual points and content types you want to include.

For Shortstack, let's make an outline of the homepage. We don't need to cover all of the content types up front, so we'll keep the homepage focused on the essentials. We'll put important secondary information that we want on every page—like navigation links and contact info—into the header and footer. Here's what the rough outline could look like:

> Header: Shortstack Books, navigation links (About, Blog, Shop)
> Featured books in the shop
> Upcoming events
> Footer: address, contact info, newsletter

We might also want to highlight recent posts from the blog, or leave those tucked away. Let's keep it simple for now and turn the outline into a workable sketch.

Sketch it out

To structure your piece, it's a good idea to practice writing modularly. Treat each paragraph or section as a building block. Write them individually, and build on your ideas as you go. Modular writing lets you focus on one concept at a time and reshuffle things when you need to. It also gives your team more room for creativity, since designers and developers can play with the structure.

At an abstract level, web content is made up of different modules of text, listed here from smallest to largest:

- Letters and characters
- Words
- Sentences
- Paragraphs
- Sections

- Articles
- Pages
- Flows
- Websites
- Systems

Like a set of matryoshka dolls, each module belongs to a larger one. **Figure 3.1** shows how these modules can relate to one another in different sketches.

DESKTOP   TABLET   PHONE

FIGURE 3.1 Each sketch presents information in a different order or hierarchy. Modules with the same priority fit side-by-side, like pieces of a puzzle.

Give your writing a shape like this to help you plan it out. Just make it up and go from there. It doesn't have to be fancy. (If you've worked with wireframes, this is a simpler version of that.)

Sketch each of the modules on your outline with squiggly lines and rectangles. Imagine how long each one needs to be, based on the available space and what the reader needs to know. If a particular section needs to include images or links, draw those in with boxes or lines.

Making this sketch will help you structure the writing for yourself. A blank screen is intimidating, so give yourself a place to start. Don't worry about the layout or the final order of things. The point of sketching is to list the elements in a visual way so that you can refer to them and move them around as you write, instead of trying to hold everything in your mind at once.

If anything feels less important or secondary, give it less space or put it lower on the page. For example, for Shortstack, events are not the most important part of the website. That module should come after the featured books, since books are the heart of the business. We need to introduce the shop and show people some of those beautiful children's books. **Figure 3.2** shows a sketch of the modules for Shortstack.

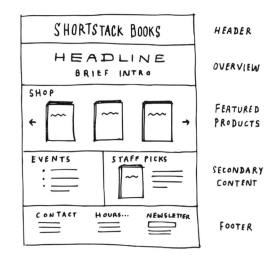

FIGURE 3.2 Here's one way we could stack it up.

Again, this is a writing plan, and not a page layout. Get the important points down and into a logical order so you can write the copy.

Write a rough draft

Now that you have a general idea of what's going on the Shortstack homepage, you can take your sketch and write a rough draft. When you do this for your own site, you'll end up with a mix of real copy and placeholder copy.

Here's what that could look like for Shortstack:

Shortstack Books

- Blog

- About

- Shop

- Brief headline announcing the shop launch

Featured books in the shop

- Book 1, title, author

- Book 2, title, author

- Book 3, title, author

Upcoming events

- Event 1, date, title

- Event 2, date, title

Shortstack Books

- Visit the shop: 111 Ellsworth Ave, Pittsburgh, PA

- Hours: 10 am to 8 pm, 7 days a week

- Weekly newsletter

This is a solid place to start. From here, you can start writing the individual blurbs and filling in the details. If you're working with a designer, this is a good time to share placeholder copy so they can start working on the layout. Including estimated word counts may help too.

Put the plan into action

At this point, you have a plan, a structure, and some working copy. Now you can focus on writing. Work through the modules, one sentence at a time. They'll grow up to be sections, pages, and flows, which eventually become entire websites. Then, tie them all together with your voice and tone.

Chapter Four

WRITING BASICS

YOU'VE DONE YOUR RESEARCH. You have a plan. You can't escape it any longer. It's time to sit down and write (eek!). Yes, this is the hard part. Hang in there, though. We're in this together. In this chapter, we'll cover:

- Basic guidelines
- Common mistakes
- Tips for getting unstuck
- Exercises for improving your writing

Let's start with a few guidelines for good writing to help you produce it.

Basic guidelines

Good writing is clear, useful, and friendly. Some sentences may be a little plain or *just the facts, ma'am*, but that's okay. A straightforward tone rarely hurts the reading experience, as long as the information is accurate.

The hardest part, of course, is making sense to someone outside your own head. To write clearly, you need to understand your subject, organize your thoughts, and present each point in a logical way. That takes a combination of research, patience, and clearheaded thinking. Style is another important layer that we'll touch on here and explore in upcoming chapters. Your style is there to help you convey your message, which means it's secondary to the message itself.

So let's get to good first and bring in style later. Good means solid, not glamorous, cute, or catchy. Practice these guidelines regularly:

- Be clear.
- Be concise.
- Be honest.
- Be considerate.
- Write how you speak.

Let's work through each of them individually. Rules and guidelines can be a little dry, but we'll try to make this enjoyable.

Be clear

Writing is almost always about clarity. Of course you want to be clear! But if you're under a deadline, it can be hard to spot what's confusing to readers. Here are a few practical tips.

Remember that you're the expert

Don't assume that readers will understand what you're writing about. You know your business and your website better than they do. Invite them in as if you're striking up a conversation or telling a story. You don't have to dumb things down, but you do need to help readers skim and follow along. Think about what you'd tell a friend or a neighbor if they were learning about the topic you're covering.

Keep it simple

If there's a shorter word to say what you mean, use it (**Table 5.1**).

TABLE 5.1 Use short, simple words

Longer	Better
compose, author	write
discover	find
incentivize	encourage, reward
objective	goal
obtain	get
optimize	improve
purchase, acquire	buy
retain	keep
utilize, leverage	use

If you have to use a technical term that people may not recognize, briefly define it or explain it in plain language.

Keep your writing as close to speech as possible. One way to do that is to read your work aloud and see if it sounds like you. For example, do you ever hear people say "inimitable" or "natch" in person? Yikes. If it feels forced, rephrase it. Another way to write like you talk is to use contractions, which crop up naturally in conversation.

Be specific

If you're writing instructions for a series of steps, go through the steps yourself and write down the names of links or buttons exactly as you see them. Be explicit in what you're asking the reader to do.

Avoid vague instructions:

> Update your settings to receive fewer communications from us.

Instead, include specific labels:

> To receive fewer emails, go to Settings > Email Notifications.

Names and labels improve clarity like signs on a highway. Show people how to get around by adding these details. This is especially important for links to articles, headings, and help content. Consider these questions as you write:

- What is the reader trying to do?
- What does the reader need to know?
- What's missing?
- What happens next?
- Is this topic covered somewhere else?

Tell readers what to expect and guide them through the process. Don't stop at a basic confirmation:

> Your order was successful.

Instead, add details about the order:

> Thanks for your order. You'll receive an email confirmation within a few minutes. [View Order] [Print Receipt]

If something goes wrong, politely explain what to do next, whether it's reading an article, resetting a password, or asking for help. Including buttons and links can help you with that.

Be consistent

Use names and labels consistently. If you refer to *notifications* in one place, call them *notifications* everywhere else—not push notifications, instant notifications, real-time alerts, or messages. Being consistent and being repetitive aren't the same thing. Consistent names reduce the number of things your readers have to remember. Being consistent helps people understand the different parts of your website and shows them where to find what they're looking for. As an added bonus, consistent terms improve usability and reduce translation costs.

You should also be consistent with how you capitalize headings and subheadings—whether you decide to use title casing or sentence casing.

Be careful with pronouns, too. Some websites are confusing in this way. They refer to the reader as *you* in one place and *me* in another. Here are a few common examples from headings and links:

> About us
>
> My account
>
> Enter your comment
>
> Your orders

Who's *us* here? Generally, *us* and *we* should refer to your company, with *our* referring to things belonging to your company. This is where *my* is especially weird. Who's *me* here? The reader or the company? One way to avoid this awkwardness is to avoid pronouns in the first place:

> About
>
> Account
>
> Enter a comment
>
> Order history

Otherwise, we recommend calling the reader *you* to keep your writing conversational. This is definitely a style choice, but you should be consistent one way or another to avoid confusion.

Break the rules thoughtfully

Most of the time, your writing should fit in with your house style or the style of the publication you're contributing to. But every now and then, you'll need to break the rules. It's common for web writers to break traditional style conventions, because some rules don't read well online. For example, most style guides say to spell out numbers up to ten, but digits usually work better on the web since readers are scanning. Another example is how you refer to people after introducing them. Traditionally, you'd use the person's last name, but people don't talk like that in person, so it's a good rule to break.

As you write, keep the appropriate rules and style conventions in mind. Be careful not to confuse or distract the reader. When in doubt, talk about the issue with an editor, rephrase the sentence, or break the rule thoughtfully. If you find yourself breaking the same rule regularly, it may be worth updating your style guide. (We'll talk about style guides and other exceptions in Chapter 12: Style Guides.)

Avoid abbreviations and acronyms

It can be tempting to shorten words to save space, but clarity should always come first. As an example, *security code* is a little longer than *CVV*, but it's easier to understand at first glance when you're talking about credit cards. If you have to use an acronym, briefly define it in plain language on the first mention.

If you're working within character or word limits, you may need to shorten words occasionally. Here are a few commonly accepted examples:

Dates: Sat Nov 22
Times: 3h5m, 3hr 5min, am, pm
Places: USA, UK, EU, JP, CA
Numbers: $20M, 45 ft, 60 m, 60 mi
Technical terms: 3G, LTE, EDGE, Wi-Fi
Formats: CD, DVD, JPG, GIF

If you decide to use abbreviations, look out for confusing ones, especially those that can refer to both states and countries. For example, CA could be either California or Canada. Use abbreviations sparingly, and add approved ones to your style guide.

Be concise

Most of the time, shorter is better. The easiest way to condense your writing is to give it a clear structure. Sketching is one way to do that. Here are a few other tips for organizing your thoughts.

Start with the main idea

Think about what people need to know right away. Move that information up to the top. Don't get to the point; start with it.

Find a direct and polite way to express your idea. Talking it out with a friend or coworker can help. Record yourself if you can so you can hear how you phrase things. Ask yourself: What am I trying to say? The answer to that question is often shorter than whatever you wrote down.

Make it scannable

Pull related ideas together. Arrange similar topics into modules and sections. Then, you can easily move anything that's out of order or fill in the gaps. As your paragraphs get longer, add clear headings to them. If you want to call out any important points, use bulleted lists to summarize them. Make it easy for readers to skim, find what they need, and know what's coming next.

Use simple sentences

Break down big ideas into manageable bites. Keep your sentences as short as possible.

Avoid trailing on:

> If you haven't already done so, you can sign up for our newsletter to receive deals and special offers delivered directly to your inbox.

Instead, try paring it down:

> Sign up for our newsletter to get special offers.

Don't make people read more than they need to. Once you figure out what your point is, whittle the writing down to the essentials. Here's another wordy example:

> For assistance with questions not listed above, please click here to see our contact information.

Instead, cut the extra words:

> Other questions? Contact us.

Cover one idea at a time. If you need to include secondary information, try linking to it instead of summarizing or repeating yourself.

Talk to your readers

Use the imperative when it's appropriate. Talk *to* your readers, not *at* them. Tell them what to do in a kind and straightforward way. This little change in perspective can help you be concise.

For example, avoid talking about yourself:

> For the holidays, our customers can find the perfect children's books on our website.

> We're excited to announce that we are introducing over 30 new products to our shop for the holidays.

Instead, be direct:

> Find the perfect holiday gift. Shop now.

> There are over 30 new items in the shop today! See what's on sale.

Be careful with the passive voice, where the subject of the sentence comes after the object:

> You have received a gift card from Maria.

Instead, use the active voice:

> Maria sent you a gift card.

Balance being direct with being nice. Huddle your nouns and verbs close together to shorten your sentences. Active verbs help you write concisely and invigorate your prose so that it feels more like a conversation.

Be positive

Be careful with negative language, which is usually longer and less friendly than positive language. Avoid telling readers what they can't do:

> You cannot continue without signing in.

Instead, be positive or neutral:

> Sign in to continue.

And while it's generally best to avoid the passive voice, in certain situations it helps you sound softer without adding too many words. It's especially useful for time-sensitive messages like payment confirmations and error messages. Directness can sometimes sound terse or robotic:

> We couldn't authorize your credit card. We cancelled your order.

In those cases, soften the language:

> We were unable to authorize your credit card. Your order has been cancelled.

Conciseness is a trickier concept, because it isn't always appropriate. You may need to vary the lengths of your sentences to keep them friendly. If you use several short sentences in a row, you can end up sounding sharp or stiff. It's also possible to cut too much, to oversimplify a complicated issue, or to reduce your message to something generic. Find the simplest way to say what you mean without losing important details.

Be honest

For web writers, honesty means two things: presenting the facts and being true to your company. It's a combination of accuracy and sincerity. Tell the truth and be nice. Don't brag about how great you are. Focus on your strengths and present them carefully. People will know when you're lying to them. Don't say an offer is "Just for you" if you're sending it to hundreds of readers.

Be careful

Along with checking for errors, you should also make sure your work is trustworthy and reliable. Back up your claims with facts and concrete examples. Don't exaggerate or overpromise. For example, if it takes an hour to purchase something over the phone, don't say it's a quick call. Or, if you're specifying how many readers you have, don't lie about the number.

Check your facts and sources. When reading through a draft, pick out any details you consider to be facts and verify them. If you're citing another writer's work or referencing a study, link to it. When you've done your research, it will come through in your writing.

Tell the truth

Make sure your writing speaks the whole truth and nothing but the truth. Even if you have the best intentions, little white lies can sometimes sneak in. Be especially aware of this when you're writing marketing copy. If you're trying to persuade people to do something, it's tempting to say things that sound nice but aren't exactly true. As Anne Lamott says, take out the lies and the boring parts.[1]

1 https://twitter.com/ANNELAMOTT/status/440540092629655552

Check in with your own feelings regularly. As you're working on each sentence, make sure the writing is sincere. It should represent your real feelings or attitude on the topic. If you feel like you're pretending or forcing specific words into a phrase, you may need to pull the language back toward reality.

Be careful with adjectives and modifiers. It's easy to overuse descriptive words and leave readers feeling unsatisfied. Replace fluffy modifiers with concrete ideas. Here are a few examples to avoid:

amazing	memorable
artisanal	natural
beautiful	powerful
dynamic	revolutionary
industry-leading	unique
innovative	everyone's favorite
intuitive	it's never been easier

Show readers how your product is different or why it's great; don't *tell* them how to feel. Avoid being melodramatic:

> With our intuitive design tools creating the site you've always wanted is easier than you ever imagined. (www.godaddy.com)

Instead, add honest, useful details:

> Choose from simple templates or customize your site over FTP.

Point out specific things you can do for the reader, instead of assuming you know what they want.

Be considerate

Help people on their own terms. Use words they understand, and treat them with the same level of respect you'd give them in person.

Be polite

Most of the time, the easiest way to show your empathy is to write how you speak. How would you talk about this in person? Make it sound more like a conversation. Show your thoughtfulness. Make the reader smile. You can even give them a little encouragement. Put yourself in the reader's shoes and check your tone to make sure you're being polite. If you need the reader to wait for a moment or fill in extra form fields, a simple "please" or "thank you" goes a long way.

Be inclusive

The words you choose affect how people relate to you and define your relationships. Keep the language open when you can. Watch out for words that turn people off or only make sense to a particular audience. Don't assume that your readers are all from the same place, age group, or industry circle.

Be careful with idioms and slang

Jokes, metaphors, regional expressions, and cultural references don't always translate well. Your readers may live in different countries, or English may not be their first language. The next time you're explaining something with a metaphor or a reference, ask yourself if there's a more universal way to make your point.

Avoid jargon and catchphrases

Don't complicate your ideas with business or industry jargon. Not everyone will understand your lingo, even if you and your boss talk that way around the office. Whenever you're reading over your work, remember to cut the bullshit (**Table 5.2**).

You probably have your own set of professional terms too. Make a list of overused words and phrases from your industry and add them to your style guide so that your team knows to avoid them.

TABLE 5.2 Jargon

Blogs and magazines	Startups
bespoke	adaptive
curate	crushing it or killing it
gifted, gifting	disruptive
sustainable	ecosystem
tweeps	engagement
X is the new Y	game changer
the future of X	impact
viral	seamless

Be respectful of personal names and genders

Use a person's chosen name and preferred gender pronoun. If you're unsure of what to call someone, use their name or consider using the singular *they*. Neutral pronouns like *them* and *they* are inclusive of all gender presentations, and considerate of the fact that not everyone identifies as male or female. Here's an example:

> Your gift card recipient can choose exactly what they want.

We use the singular *they* throughout this book for that reason and because it sounds less awkward than the alternatives. And while it may be a controversial topic for grammarians, the singular *they* has been in use since the 1300s.

Okay, those are all the rules for now. Still here? Great! To sum it up, good content presents the facts in a kind, honest, appropriate way.

Getting unstuck

So far, we've covered the basics of good writing and looked at some examples. But if you're feeling stuck on the writing itself, you may need a little push in the right direction. Here are a few things to try:

Be patient. The hardest part of writing is waiting for the right words to come to mind. Keep at it. Stay in your chair, and be kind to yourself as you work through drafts. Don't try to write and edit at the same time. The first draft is usually the most painful, but don't be discouraged by that. Writing is a process, and like anything worth doing, it takes time.

Switch it up. Depending on what you're writing, it may be easier to start on one piece than another. If you're stuck, try switching over to a different page or section. You can also try talking it out with a friend. You don't have to go in order. In fact, we usually save the introduction for last.

Clear your head. If your brain isn't cooperating, take a walk or try writing in a different environment. Give yourself time to think it through before you force words onto the page. Sometimes all you need is a change of scenery.

Read edited text. Reading is the best way to get better at writing. Study other people's work. Books and magazines can expand your vocabulary and help you develop an ear for strong sentences. As you read, you'll start to notice different styles, which can help you develop your own voice.

There's a world of wonderful writing advice out there. We've included a list of our favorite books in the Further Reading section.

Go further

After you finish a first or second draft, take a break and let your work rest overnight. Look at it tomorrow with fresh eyes. Ask a few friends or fellow writers for an outside opinion. Find ways to push your writing a little further.

Try different options

One thing you can do to improve your copy is to come up with a few variations. This can help you explore a specific idea in the copy or find the best way to express it. Try words and phrases with slightly different meanings. Think of different directions you could take the feeling or essence of the word. As an example, here are some variations on a button label:

Post	Comment	Share
Publish	Send	Save

Which one works best? How are they different? Along with different words and phrases, try variations in length. Here are some examples for a nonprofit:

Donate	Make a donation
Donate now	Save a life today
Give back	Help us save lives
Fund a project	Join the fight. Make a contribution.

Longer labels may work better as links or headlines. Write alternate versions to find the best words for your audience. A visual thesaurus or online tool like Wordnik (www.wordnik.com) is a great resource for this.

For longer sections of text, switch the order of your main points. Here's a basic example using the same button label:

Get the best deals on zippers.
Join Zipzip by creating an account.

[Create account]

Create an account.
Get the best deals on zippers.

[Create account]

Presenting a few options can be especially helpful if you're part of a team. Most people aren't content experts, and it may be hard to know what they're expecting from you. Show your team some copy variations to get them involved and speed up the decision-making process. This is also a great starting point for running simple tests on your content.

Read on

People will read your work in different places, on different devices, and in different formats. They could be reading on a phone, or tablet, or computer. They could be on a train commuting to work, eating dinner, or relaxing on the couch. Read your writing in different contexts, so you can experience it the same way. And if you wrote the text in a word processor, be sure to read it online after you publish it.

Check your work

Read your writing on paper too. This is useful for improving drafts, spotting typos, and checking your tone. Tape your current draft to a whiteboard, or find a quiet corner to sit down and read. If you're feeling adventurous, grab a pen (any color will do) and go to town. For longer pieces, you can check the structure by cutting pages and paragraphs into strips and reordering the sections. As you read, listen to how the words sound and consider each point you're making. Keep an eye out for redundant ideas. Check for the basics: Are there typos? Are there clunky sentences? Does it all make sense? Would links or references help the reader? Take some time to reread and reconsider your work.

Ask for feedback

We all get too close to our writing. Ask a friend or coworker you respect to read over your draft. We call these people *early readers*. It might feel embarrassing to share unfinished work, especially earlier in the process, but it can dramatically improve your writing.

Tell your early reader what kind of feedback you're expecting. Does it make sense? Does it flow? Is it interesting? Are there any gaps? Does it sound like you? Or, you may have more specific questions about themes or details in the piece. Be clear about what you need from your early reader and respectful of their time. You may need to move things around or make other changes afterwards, but it's better to learn that early in the process. Talking about your writing is a great way to make it clear, concise, and polished. (For more editing tips, see Chapter 11: The Revision Process.)

Edit it live

Try editing an existing piece of text in its real habitat. We love this little trick! It's helpful in meetings where you're debating headlines or labels with your team. It's also helpful for copyediting on your own. And it's easier than you might think. Let's look at two ways to edit your text in context.

Inspect element

Open the page in your browser. Right-click the text you want to edit. Choose Inspect Element in the pop-up menu. The text should be highlighted in the source code. Replace it with something new. Press the Return key to see what the page would look like with the new text. If you want to show a few variations before making the changes, take a screenshot of each one.

Use Keynote or PowerPoint

Open the page in your browser. Take a screenshot of it at the appropriate size (small for mobile, larger for tablet, and so on). Drop the screenshot into a blank presentation slide in Keynote or PowerPoint. Add a text box over the current text. Give it a background color that matches the background of your site. For example, if the background is white and the text is blue, make the background of the new text box white. Then, write over the image in blue text with the copy you're trying out.

Make a reverse outline

You probably remember making outlines in school. To outline something, you typically write a list of things you want to say, put them in order, and then expand on each of the list items. To review longer pieces of text, try making an outline after you have a draft (we call this *reverse outlining*). Pull the main ideas from what you wrote into bullets or headers. This can give you a sense of what you've covered and what's missing. It can also help you see larger themes in your writing and show you where you might need to move things around. This is also a great time to review the labels and headings you chose to guide readers through your piece.

Keep practicing

As you work through drafts, keep pushing toward being clear, concise, considerate, and honest. In the next two chapters, we'll show you how to write like you speak and bring your voice to the page.

Chapter Five

FIND YOUR VOICE

Your voice is in the fiber of your communications. It's what makes people feel like they're listening to someone they know when they visit your website. It should come from a real place.

People often use the words *voice* and *tone* interchangeably, but they're not the same thing. Your *voice* is your company's public personality. It doesn't change much from day to day. Like your own individual personality, it comes through in all of your content and influences how people perceive you. On the other hand, your *tone* changes to fit the situation. While your voice is more about you, your tone is about your readers and how they feel. Together, your voice and tone make up your writing style. We'll get into tone in the next chapter, but let's start with finding your voice.

In this chapter, we'll discuss how to:

- Find your voice and translate it to the page
- Pick a few useful brand attributes
- Choose the right words to talk about your company

We'll also show you some exercises to help you through this process and get your teammates and contributors on board.

Look inward

A voice is a reflection of the people behind it. Your company exists for a reason, maybe because you want to make the world a better place or make people's lives a little easier. Your perspective is unique to your brand. Your company is different from its competitors, and your voice shows people how you're different.

Great voices share these qualities:

- They put customers first.
- They reflect the company's culture.
- They're lively, human, and appropriate.
- They don't sacrifice clarity for personality.
- They evolve over time.

Your voice is what makes all of your communications sound like they came from the same place. If you read something and think, "That doesn't sound like us!" or "Nobody would say that in real life," then your voice is probably off. That's the kind of problem you can solve by working to define your style, voice, and tone.

This higher-level editorial work isn't an optional part of the process. Your voice directly affects everything you write. And because voice is an intrinsic part of any brand's identity, it also shapes design principles, sets the bar for customer service, and even influences the way people communicate around the office.

Brands are not people

Companies are not people. They're *made of* people—and that's an important distinction. When we refer to *brand voice* in this book, we're talking about a voice that's an honest reflection of the people behind your company or website.

There's a lot of advice out there about inventing a voice for your brand, as if you're developing a character for a novel or a play. Avoid that. You're not here to entertain people. Your writing needs to come from real experiences and genuine conversations. A fictional voice can be fun for a minute, but it ultimately comes off as disingenuous (mostly because it is). It's also a lot to keep up with! If you're not writing from a real place, it's hard to get it right every time. Besides, if your voice is phony, you'll have the added pressure of staying in character. Your voice should feel as natural for you as talking to a reader or customer in person. Articulating your voice will help you keep your content consistent as your company grows.

Your brand voice should reflect your company's values, and it should be appropriate for your industry. It probably doesn't make sense for a bank to be too goofy, or for a pet store to be super sophisticated. And don't feel pressured to be funny or hip just because other companies are doing it. That never ends well.

Along the same lines, there's no need to use the royal "we" on your About page if you're not working on a team. If you write, edit, and publish everything on your blog, be proud of that! Own it. Write in the first person, and let your readers get to know the real you. Before you publish anything, get into the habit of asking yourself, "Does this sound like me?"

Make an effort

Have you ever thought for hours about the subjectivity and nuance of words, or read a sentence over and over in your head because something just didn't feel right? If you're like us, you've probably stared at an email more than once, trying to decide if the exclamation mark after "thanks" seems friendly or flippant. That's what it means to care deeply about your voice and tone. This sort of attention to language enriches your content and makes you a more valuable team member—whether or not you're a professional writer. Developing an honest voice is the best way to keep your communications appropriate and connect with your readers on a human level.

Keep the spirit

When you're ready to explore your voice, your starting point will depend on your website and the existing content you're dealing with. If you're working on a brand with an established voice, then ask around to see if there's already a style guide or brand guidelines. In that case, your job might be to wrap your head around it and start writing. If you're working with a growing business, it could be time to reevaluate the voice and personality. Or maybe you've already identified your company's voice, and you need to get it all on paper to help writers understand it. If you're starting from scratch, we'll cover that too.

Established brands already have lots of public content, so voice work can be an overwhelming process. Before you dig in, find your way back to the company's roots. Read as much as you can in chronological order: blog posts, older versions of the website, comments from customers, whatever you can get your hands on. Notice what's changed over time. Pay attention to what *hasn't* changed, too. That will get you thinking about how the language should evolve, and what needs to stay the same.

As you take in all of this information, identify the themes and obvious messages. Look for conflicts between them. If at one point the company's focus shifted from "simple and fun" to "powerful and advanced," find out why. Maybe the change was intentional—or maybe a new writer perceived the brand voice differently than the original writer. The more you read, the better you'll understand these problems and shifts in context.

If you work for yourself, remember why you started your company or website in the first place. Try to relive your excitement about the adventure, and think about the people you wanted to serve. In the early stages, you were probably more focused on building a community than the bottom line. You were writing to early adopters, instead of the general public. Tap into that energy to discover (or rediscover) your company's voice. If you're working for a new company started by someone else, then pull up a chair and have the founder take you back to the start.

Keep your mind open during your research and interviews. Don't rush through it. Talk about your discoveries, and get all your questions answered. You'll probably notice some of the same words coming up again and again.

Find the right words

The language that relates to your company is a combination of two things: the words you use to describe yourself and the words customers or readers use to describe you. Ideally, you've chosen language that people can understand and relate to, so your customers are using the same kinds of words. It's exciting to see people using the same language you use to talk about yourself or your products. If you notice a gap, it might be time to reconsider how you're communicating. It could be an internal problem or a sign that your communication style doesn't fit your audience. It could also be that there's an uncomfortable difference between the company's marketing message and the customer experience. If people around the office are confused or sending conflicting messages, your public content will reflect that.

Listening is half the battle. Sit down with your teammates or clients to understand how they perceive the brand. If you're already doing internal interviews as part of your process, that's a great time to slip in voice and tone work without increasing the scope of a project much. If the founder or CEO is available to you, set up an interview. Nine times out of ten, that's the closest you'll get to the heart of the company.

Ask yourself and your colleagues these questions:

- Why did you start this company? What led you to the idea?
- What do you know about our readers? What do they care about?
- Who do you see as our competition? How are we different?
- What does success mean for us? Where do you want to take our customers?

- How do you want people to feel when they visit our website or use our products?
- Are there any associations we should avoid?

Look for emotional responses during interviews. Take notes about people's gut reactions, moments when their eyes light up, and things that make them smile or laugh. If they seem like they really want to talk about something, let them ramble. Take it all in. Embrace any silences, too, because sometimes the best answers come after a long pause. Those responses are little glimpses of someone's true personality—and the company's culture.

Listen carefully to your customers, too. Sit in on user research interviews, or conduct your own. Search Twitter, Facebook, and blog posts to find out how people talk about your brand, and how that compares to the company's identity. Which words do they use? If you see yourself as playful and eccentric but customers keep calling you boring on Twitter, you've got a communication problem. If you like what they're saying about you, then reflect their words and phrases in your copy. That keeps your writing conversational and relevant.

As you read up on the company and talk to people around the office, soak up everything. Make time for unstructured interviews and spur-of-the moment conversations. Stop by people's desks if you work in-house. Listen hard during meetings, and write down memorable words and phrases. Get it all on paper.

Make a This But Not That list

One of our favorite tools for developing a brand voice is what we call a This But Not That list. It's easy: List some words that describe your brand, and then explain each one by what it *doesn't* mean. That second word helps writers better understand each personality trait.

For example, here's MailChimp's list:

MailChimp is...

Fun but not childish

Clever but not silly

Confident but not cocky

Smart but not stodgy

Cool but not alienating

Informal but not sloppy

Helpful but not overbearing

Expert but not bossy

Weird but not inappropriate

And here's what our fictional bookstore's This But Not That list might look like:

Shortstack Books is...

Childlike but not immature

Fanciful but not ridiculous

Educational but not academic

Curious but not confused

Optimistic but not sappy

Encouraging but not gushing

Make a list like this for your company. Add it to your brand guidelines or style guide so everyone who communicates on behalf of the company is on the same page. You could also include it in a new-employee handbook. Keep these attributes handy as you continue to develop your style.

Margot Bloomstein's card sorting exercise

Margot Bloomstein is a brand and content strategy consultant, and the author of *Content Strategy at Work*. She uses a card-sorting activity to help her clients find their brand's personality and include the whole team in the conversation. She starts by spreading out a bunch of index cards, each labeled with a brand attribute. Here are some examples of the attributes she includes:

cool	cutting-edge
down-to-earth	timeless
innovative	wise
conservative	empowering
professional	progressive
eclectic	formal
savvy	trendy
approachable	casual
classic	elite

Then, she invites her clients (including decision makers, copywriters, designers, and creative directors) to work together to sort them into three categories: who we are, who we'd like to be, and who we're not. After that, they remove the least useful attributes and refine the list. Once they've narrowed it down, they get rid of the "who we're not" category and talk about the other two. (You could hang on to those negative attributes though, in case they're useful for your This But Not That list.)

Margot says the activity directly influences a company's messages and opens up conversations about organizational goals. "At a basic level, it encourages clients to interact with their brand in a very hands-on way. Participants are picking up terms, considering them against other terms, and making tough choices about what they can toss out or leave behind," she says. "For anyone who's ever said, 'We can't put everything on the homepage,' or 'We can't communicate everything at the same time,' you know the value of these trade-offs."

Keep at it

These tips and exercises will help you articulate your brand voice and teach it to other people, but voice work never ends. As your company grows, your voice will need to change in subtle ways to reflect that. Understanding where you are and where you want to be is the first step to writing with purpose. Learning how to talk to your customers in a genuine way is especially important for growing companies, because adding individual voices to the mix can muddle the overall message. Keep your voice close to your mission. And when in doubt, write from the heart.

Chapter Six

WATCH YOUR TONE

THINK ABOUT HOW YOU TALK with your best friend when you're joking around. Maybe you're informal, silly, or sarcastic. Now, imagine how you'd talk to the president or the queen if you had the chance. You'd probably be a little more formal, right? That's because you naturally adapt your tone to fit the situation. Most of us do this without even thinking about it, to make other people feel comfortable. This shift in tone is part of our everyday lives, but it's not always present in our writing.

When you're talking to someone face-to-face, you can make eye contact with them and watch their expressions. That gives you a sense of how they might be feeling, or what kind of mood they're in. If they're distracted or stressed, you probably talk to them in a softer way than if they're in a good mood. But you don't have the benefit of body language online, so you have to find other ways to show people you're listening. In this chapter, we'll explore different ways to do that.

We'll cover how to:

- Show empathy in your writing
- Map your content types to your readers' feelings
- Adapt your tone to different situations
- Be sensitive when it comes to humor

The first step is to think about how your readers may be feeling, based on the type of content you're writing.

Show your empathy

By now, you should have a list of content types that you publish. Each one addresses a specific goal, audience, or problem. To connect with people and show you care, you have to adapt your style to fit their needs at the very moment they're reading your content.

Think about the situation your readers are in. What did they come here for? Blog posts can be personal and casual, but if you're writing a technical document to help someone troubleshoot, you probably need to take on an instructional tone. You can be a little more dramatic or persuasive in a marketing campaign than in your help center. Understanding the purpose behind each of your content types will help you keep the writing useful and appropriate for your readers.

Above all, when you're thinking about tone, consider the context of the message. For example, if you're giving directions, you can naturally assume that readers need help finding their way. Making a joke or talking about yourself may not be appropriate there.

Second that emotion

The next step is to think about your reader's emotional state. Try to understand their frame of mind and talk to them where they are.

Find out what happens just before your message appears. Is this good news that will make readers feel happy, relieved, or excited, or is it bad news that will make them frustrated, angry, or upset? Will the message brighten their day, or put them in a difficult situation? Are readers prepared, or will they be caught off guard? These questions will help you decide how to write the message.

Go through your list of content types and map them to your reader's emotional state. Next to each content type, write down three or four emotions that people could be feeling in the moment. We recommend Plutchik's wheel of emotions as a reference (**Figure 6.1**). This classic model illustrates a range of feelings and emotional states, showing how they relate to one another.

FIGURE 6.1 A variation on Plutchik's wheel of emotions.

As you match things up, you'll probably find yourself writing down emotions from all over the wheel. **Table 6.1** shows how you might map things out for your research or your style guide.

TABLE 6.1 Content mapping

Content type	Reader's emotional state	Appropriate tone
Error message	Confusion, stress, anger	Gentle, calm, serious
Help document	Confusion, annoyance	Straightforward, helpful
Blog post	Interest, anticipation, curiosity	Casual, friendly

continues

TABLE 6.1 Content mapping *(continued)*

Content type	Reader's emotional state	Appropriate tone
Success message	Relief, pride, joy	Positive, friendly, enthusiastic
Legal document	Stress, confusion, annoyance	Clear, serious, straightforward
Email newsletter	Interest, curiosity, distraction	Enthusiastic, helpful, personal
Marketing campaign	Surprise, delight, distraction	Enthusiastic, memorable

If you're writing bad news like an error message or out-of-stock notification, then err on the serious side. These types of messages can make people feel stressed or frustrated. Explain the situation clearly and get right to the point. Do your best to avoid causing any added frustration.

On the other hand, if you're writing good news like an announcement or order confirmation, it's okay to be more casual. People are likely to be in a positive frame of mind in those places. You can delight your readers and show your personality—as long as you're clearly communicating the important details too.

Think about how you'd behave in a face-to-face conversation, and put yourself in the reader's shoes. If you were congratulating someone on a job well done, you might take on a lighthearted and enthusiastic tone. But if you were giving someone a speeding ticket, you'd get right to the point and save the jokes for later.

Let's look at two examples for Shortstack Books. We'd use an upbeat tone when an order ships, but play it straight if something was out of stock:

Yay! Your book is on the way.

We're sorry. That book is out of stock. Would you like to be notified when it's available?

For another example of how tone and context fit together, let's look at the word "oops" in two different scenarios. First, an error message:

> Oops! We can't seem to find this page.

Here "oops" is a friendly way to soften the message and apologize without being, well, overly apologetic. This message strikes a nice tone. A broken link isn't a big deal, so this news probably won't ruin someone's day. But what if we use the same exclamation in an account suspension notice?

> Oops! Your account has been suspended due to a high complaint rate.

That innocent little word reads quite differently in this example. An account suspension notice could ruin someone's day or even get them fired. This isn't the place for casual language or cuteness. And that alarming exclamation mark makes the message seem even more tone deaf. Make sure you're using appropriate words and that your tone fits the situation.

A voice and tone guide can help you teach these concepts to other writers. MailChimp's guide (http://voiceandtone.com) lists the different content types on the website, so writers know what to say in each part of the interface. Each entry includes a hypothetical quote from the reader, emotions they might be feeling, a sample response, and writing tips. MailChimp uses this voice and tone guide as an extension of the house style guide. People reference it to see how to show empathy in their writing.

Read your work aloud

Learn to love talking to yourself, because reading your work out loud will transform your writing. When you're not sure if you're striking the right tone, read your content aloud to see how it sounds. Peter Elbow, professor emeritus of English at the University of Massachusetts at Amherst, calls this "speaking onto the page."

In his book *Vernacular Eloquence*, he says:

> A good teacher I know, Jenifer Auger, has a simple but effective technique for the writing classroom. When her students have blah voiceless writing, she makes them speak the following words to her before reading their text: "*Listen* to me, I have something to tell you."[1]

There are two times during the writing process when it's especially useful to talk it out. The first is before you even start writing. Pretend someone is asking you a question and talk out the answer. If you're writing an About section for your blog, then answer the question: "What's your blog like?" out loud, as if you're chatting with someone at a party. Then, transcribe what you said. If you can record yourself or use speech-to-text software, that'll help you in the process.

Get your responses down in all their messy glory. From there, refine what you said. Remove the ums and uhs and maybes and sos. Little by little, make your sentences more concise. This is a simple way to keep your writing conversational.

The second time to read your work aloud is after finishing a draft. As you read, do what we call a *human check*. Listen for awkward constructions and phrases that you wouldn't say in conversation. If you get to a part where you think, "Hmm, this isn't sitting right," or "Eek! That wasn't very nice," revise the sentence and read it again. Keep revising and reading aloud until it's better.

It's also helpful to have a friend or coworker read your work out loud *to you*. This may feel a little awkward at first, but hearing someone else read the words gets you outside your own head and into your reader's shoes.

When you're writing, try to picture one of your readers sitting beside you. Maybe you're at your kitchen table or meeting somewhere you feel comfortable. Think about how the reader got here and how you can make their day a little brighter.

---

1 Peter Elbow, *Vernacular Eloquence: What Speech Can Bring to Writing*. (New York: Oxford University Press, 2012), 254.

GOV.UK's inclusive tone of voice

GOV.UK provides information about government services in the United Kingdom. The audience includes everyone living in the UK—and that's a wide range of people with different backgrounds and needs. The site covers everything from calculating tax dividends to getting disability benefits to registering a birth. People come to GOV.UK looking for information that could dramatically affect their lives.

Sarah Richards, head of content design, works with her team to write helpful content that's easy to find. "We know users may not be concentrating well when these sorts of life events are happening," she says. "So not only do we have the usual readability and usability considerations like size of screen, time, and natural scanning behavior, we know we are not exactly *fun* either." GOV.UK's voice isn't quirky or cutesy because it's not appropriate for the government to act that way. The site's writers stick to the facts and use plain language, avoiding spin and jargon. They also have to keep in mind that English is a second language for many of their readers, which is another reason for them to write simply. Here are the first few sentences of a GOV.UK article called "Looking for work if you're disabled":

> When you're looking for work, look for the 'positive about disabled people' symbol (with 2 ticks) on adverts and application forms. The symbol means the employer is committed to employing disabled people. If a job advert displays the symbol, you'll be guaranteed an interview if you meet the basic conditions for the job.

It's simple, clear, and gets right to the point. "Government is complicated," says Richards. "Communicating government policy can't be; we need to make it understood by anyone interested enough to look for it."

Keep your humor in check

A sense of humor can turn onetime customers into loyal fans, but it can also turn people off. Humor is where a lot of companies miss the mark. They think that if they have a fun personality, then they should be funny *all the time*. Bad idea. As a rule, jokes don't belong in serious situations. If your company has a sense of humor, it's important to know when to keep a straight face.

Unless you're a comedian or you work for a comedy brand, your goal shouldn't be to make people laugh. Content should be useful and clear; being funny is a bonus, when it happens at the right time. Let's look at some examples of places to use humor and where to avoid it.

The good news messages we talked about earlier are safe for humor. Product descriptions are also nice places to show your company's personality, particularly for apparel, toys, and luxury items. When people are shopping for these kinds of things, they're probably excited about their purchase and ready to spend some money. Of course, if you sell insurance, medical equipment, or business software, think twice before writing a clever product page.

Woot, a daily deal company and subsidiary of Amazon, is known for its informal voice and goofy-to-sarcastic sense of humor. The writers clearly have fun with their product descriptions. Here's an excerpt about a glassware set:

> Drinking *without* drinkware is *annoying*. You can't guzzle down ice cold soda from your hands! You can't have a nice shot of whiskey from a canteen! Just suck it up and buy glassware, okay? It's part of being human.

This funny description comes after important details like the product name, specifications, price, and total discount. It's the perfect spot for humor, and the tone puts customers in a good mood while they're considering a purchase.

On the other hand, Contact Us and Frequently Asked Questions pages aren't the best places for jokes. People rarely contact a company just to say hello. More often, they have a problem or complaint. Here's how Woot answers the question, "Will I receive customer support like I'm used to?" on its FAQ page:

> If you buy something you don't end up liking or you have what marketing people call "buyer's remorse," sell it on Craigslist or at a garage sale. It's likely you'll make money doing this and save everyone a hassle. If the item doesn't work, first, find out what you're doing wrong. Yes, we know you think the item is bad, but it's probably your fault. Google your problem, or come back to that product discussion in our community and ask other people if they know. Try to call the manufacturer and ask if they know. If you give up, then go to our Support page to communicate the issue with our Customer Support Team or follow on to the next FAQ entry.[2]

The sarcasm here doesn't have quite the same effect as it does on the product page. This answer might be amusing to superfans, but it's probably irritating to new customers who need their questions answered. That's what happens when a company's tone stays the same across content types. What works well in one place comes off differently in another. And what worked with a small, passionate customer base may become off-putting as the company and its community grows.

Without facial expressions and verbal cues, it's difficult to strike the right tone when it comes to "all in good fun" sarcasm. If you're already on thin ice, your readers probably won't be charmed by your delightful sense of humor. Ask yourself whether they may be feeling stressed or frustrated. If the answer is yes, then save the jokes for later. Don't let your personality get in the way of what you're communicating.

Making fun of competitors is another common type of humor, especially in the tech world, but we don't recommend it. Microsoft faced an overwhelming amount of criticism when it launched its "Scroogled" campaign, which mocked Google's policies and practices. This kind of

---

2 http://www.woot.com/faq

humor appears desperate, and it makes a company look like the bully on the playground. Let customers come to their own conclusions about your competitors' weaknesses—or better yet, get them to focus on your strengths instead.

Whimsical wordplay is generally safe and unlikely to offend anyone. Clothing retailer ModCloth uses a pun in almost every product name (Mermaid With Love Dress, All Knit Long Dress, Ready to Glow Top). This kind of humor could get annoying fast in some crowds, but ModCloth knows its audience—young people shopping for affordable, vintage-inspired clothing—and their audience likes the puns. In fact, they like the puns *so much* that the shop has a recurring "Name It and Win It" contest, where customers can enter to name a new product. Every time ModCloth runs the contest, hundreds of customers comment with very punny dress names.

Finally, pop culture references and "nerd humor" can be fun when used sparingly and in the right context. Blog posts and social media channels are good places for this kind of thing, since they're time-stamped. If your current event reference goes out of style, that's okay—the post has a date on it. But before you make that Star Wars joke, be sure your readers know their Ewoks from their Wookies.

Don't be too formal

If you focus too closely on making your writing grammatically perfect, you may end up with stodgy content that nobody wants to read. Formality can make readers squirm, especially if they're already in an uncomfortable situation.

Try reading this error message aloud:

> We regret to inform you that this item was so popular that it has sold out.

The message is overly formal and longer than it needs to be. People don't talk that way in real life. This version is much better:

> We're sorry, this item is out of stock. Want us to email you when it's available?

Don't let your writing get in the way of your message. Again, the best way to show your empathy is to put yourself in the reader's shoes. When you sit down to write, think about the people on the other side of the screen. Who are they? What do they need to hear from you? Before you publish anything, check your tone by asking yourself these questions:

- Is it useful?
- Is it true?
- Is it nice?

If the answer to any of them is no, then you're not quite finished. The first two questions are pretty straightforward—everything you publish should serve a purpose and tell the truth. The third question addresses your voice and tone. You can't be funny all the time, and you don't even have to be interesting all the time. But you can always be nice. And that's a big deal for the people reading your work.

As you incorporate voice and tone exercises into your writing, share them with your team and contributors. Teach them to notice subtle differences in style and word choice. And if you're editing their writing, let them know why a particular phrase or sentence structure works better for your customers. Keep track of issues that come up often, so you can talk about them in workshops or in your style guide.

Chapter Seven

BUILD A COMMUNITY

COMMUNITY BUILDING is part of every writer's job. Everything you write, from the splashy copy on your homepage to your short and sweet email replies, can help you earn trust with your readers. In the early stages, you may be more focused on building a community than anything else. It takes time to find people who share your values and want to hear from you. This chapter covers how to:

- Find and nurture your community
- Write blog posts, email newsletters, and social media posts
- Stay close to your readers through growth and change

We'll talk about what it means to be community-minded, and why it's important to let readers connect with each other on their own terms.

Community matters

Let's look at the word *community*. We use it to refer to loyal readers who care what you have to say. They're the early adopters who took a chance on you. They're your return customers, the people who email you for advice, or the friendly strangers who come up to you at events.

And they're the people who follow you on Twitter, subscribe to your newsletter, and comment on your blog. A community looks different for everyone, but you know who your people are.

Know your role

Try not to think of your readers as fans or followers. That paints a picture of a one-sided relationship, which is the opposite of what you're trying to do. Community building is about making real connections with people. Sadly, many businesses think it's about getting likes on Facebook or racking up Twitter followers.

As you write, reflect on the role you play in your readers' lives. It's probably a small role, and that's okay. The more realistic you are about that, the easier it will be to meet their needs. Be part of your community too. Think of it like building a neighborhood around your house. You may have started the whole thing, but you still need to live there too.

Be present and really *listen*. Once you start forming relationships with your readers, take the time to care for those relationships. If you give people what they want, they'll keep coming back to your site, growing more comfortable with you over time. At some point, they'll know what to expect from you and trust you enough to tell their friends about you. Word-of-mouth recommendations can have more power than search results. That's how social sites like Twitter and Facebook can help your business: people trust their friends to recommend good things. Your company can tweet all day, but it will never have the same effect as people tweeting nice things about you.

Find your people

One place to begin is by going where your people are and observing them. Look up your company name or website on Twitter, Facebook, and search engines. Read what people have to say. Find reviews of your products and services. Take notes on what you learn: What are they interested in? How did they find you? What kind of language do they use to describe your company? Is it different from what you expected? This will help you get to the heart of your community.

It will also help you improve your writing in practical ways. If a lot of people find your website by looking for "easy vegetarian recipes," then you might want to, oh, post more easy vegetarian recipes. As you learn about your readers, you may notice that they have similar questions about your company. That can give you ideas about what they want to learn.

Once you have a better sense of your community, you can make your content more interesting to them. You may also find areas of confusion, which could inspire you to clarify the language on your website, improve a feature, or write new help documents.

Learn their language

See how people find your website. Look at the referrals in your analytics. That can tell you where readers are coming from, and show you how they talk about you.

When people are looking for information about your company, they'll usually search for your name and related keywords. For example, if someone is looking for a restaurant, they'll search the name of the restaurant and the neighborhood it's in or the kind of food it serves. Google calls this *co-searching*, and you can see these keywords in your analytics. The associations may surprise you. If the first keyword for your blog is architecture but you're an interior design firm, you may need to say more about interior design or label your posts clearly.

Find out what your most popular articles and pages are, and how much time people spend reading them. Maybe the titles have similar styles, or the posts touch on similar topics. Keep those insights in mind without getting too bogged down in the data. Don't let numbers inform your content on a high level, but do think about which topics, titles, and styles work for your readers.

Consider the message

Before you start writing, think about the best place to share your message. What are you trying to convey? How much do you need to say? If you're sharing detailed information and you need space for words and images, then a blog post might be your best bet. If you just want to post a quick link, social media makes more sense. But if you need to tell customers that your company is being acquired, then you should send them an email explaining what will happen with their data. It's important to make these decisions early, because they affect your approach and tone.

Now let's get into some specific types of content that will help you build a loyal community and stay close to your readers.

Blogs

Your business may have a blog, or your business may *be* your blog. Either way, your blog is a great place to speak to your community. In general, blog posts can be casual in tone. People are reading your blog because they're interested in what you have to say. There's already a level of trust there. Be friendly, and use language readers understand without dumbing anything down. We love author Neil Gaiman's advice for bloggers:

> Use your blog to connect. Use it as you. Don't "network" or "promote." Just talk.[1]

No matter what you're writing about, focus on being genuine more than polished. Talk to your readers like you'd talk to someone you know.

Develop topics

"What should I blog about?" is a question we hear a lot. If you're a professional blogger, then you already have a general topic you write about every day. From there, it's a matter of choosing subtopics,

---

1 http://publishingperspectives.com/2010/05/%E2%80%9Cconnect-dont-network-author-blog-award-winners-gaiman-benet-on-blogging/

categories, and angles—and keeping the ideas flowing. If you have a blog for your business, consider broadening your focus to your entire industry or related fields, rather than blogging exclusively about your company. Our fictional store, Shortstack Books, might publish reviews of children's literature on the company blog. A clothing boutique could cover fashion-related topics, instead of highlighting only products in the shop. You're an expert in your field, and writing about things that inspire you is a heck of a lot more interesting than talking about yourself all the time. It's difficult to get people excited about *any* company's blog, so cover topics that are genuinely interesting and useful.

Don't write posts just because you haven't blogged in a while. If you're not into it, that will come through in your writing. If you've got blogging on the brain, then you'll find yourself inspired by things you read throughout the day. Whenever that happens, make a quick note—or share a link in a tweet or Facebook post, and elaborate on your blog down the road. That's also a great way to gauge interest from your community before you commit to a topic.

Work with contributors

As your readership grows, you may want to publish more frequently or invite people to contribute to your blog. Give them a style guide with voice and tone standards (see Chapter 12: Style Guides for details), and make sure they understand your different audiences.

Give your contributors some leeway on voice and tone. People understand that when they're reading a blog, different writers may be posting there. As long as your contributors stick to your general writing principles, there's wiggle room when it comes to individual styles. Rather than having one Official Company Blogger, contributors add variety and make things more interesting for your readers.

Some companies have one writer work on every post, giving credit to different people, depending on the material. We don't recommend corporate ghostwriting, because it keeps your team from feeling involved and gives credit to someone who didn't do the writing.

Types of posts

Try a few different types of posts and see what works for you. Here are some approaches that work well across industries:

- Your blog is a good place to share **news and updates** from your headquarters. Announce events you're hosting, job openings, and new store locations.

- Product and tech companies can **highlight features and releases**. Some companies have abandoned press releases completely, since blog posts are often more effective.

- Since blog posts can have lots of photos and images, they're a good format for **step-by-step instructions** and how-to articles too.

- You could share **case studies and customer stories** to highlight cool things people are doing in your community.

- Many blogs run **ongoing series** about single topics. For example, a lifestyle blog might feature "Monday Meals" or an online store might do a weekly "Customer Spotlight."

Blogging basics

Now let's go over some tips for writing blog posts.

Write clear titles

Your titles should get people's attention and explain what the post is about in a few words. If you can make it clear *and* clever, that's even better. Avoid vague language and empty enthusiasm:

New City Guide!

Instead, add useful details to pull in the reader:

City Guide: 24 Hours in New Orleans

Stay away from annoying linkbait:

> You'll Never Believe What This Kid Does With Paper

Instead, set the reader's expectations:

> Meet Mayhem, a Four-Year-Old Fashion Designer

If you're having trouble writing headlines, skim your favorite magazines or news sites to see what catches your eye. Look at the sentence structure, and play with similar phrasing. We'll cover headlines in the next chapter.

Break up the text

Short paragraphs generally work best in blog posts. Break up the words with images, lists, and subheadings. If you have three or four consecutive paragraphs about the same topic, add a clear subheading to help people skim and scan.

Link away

Don't try to keep people on your website forever. Include links to articles and websites wherever it's appropriate. If people like your writing and the content you share, they'll come back for more.

Read the comments

When readers comment on your posts, take the time to reply to them. Let them know you're listening, and keep an eye out for questions or themes to address in another post.

Make an editorial calendar

A simple editorial calendar can help you schedule posts in advance, organize topics you want to cover on your blog or website, and keep track of multiple pieces at a time. We've seen them work as shared calendars or spreadsheets.

Here are topics we usually include:

- General info: working title, topics, categories or tags
- Details and purpose: goals, audiences, keywords, and calls to action
- Research notes: topic experts, sources, references
- Workflow: author, editors or reviewers, draft status, budget, deadlines

Even a bare-bones editorial calendar can keep your publishing schedule on track.

If you don't have anything to say, you shouldn't post anything new—but try not to let your blog go weeks and weeks without posting. People may check back a few times, and then give up on you completely. If you have time, create a backlog of posts to put up when there's a lull.

Play by the rules

Make sure you have permission to use the images you publish, and credit the artist whenever possible. If you quote someone or were inspired by another post, give that person credit and link to the source. Some sites specify how they prefer to be referenced, so check before yanking a quote without permission. Nonprofit newsroom ProPublica has a wonderful page called Steal Our Stories.[2] Anyone can republish the site's articles and graphics for free, as long as they follow a few guidelines.

Be aware of the FTC guidelines for bloggers, particularly when it comes to disclosures.[3] If you were paid to write a post, your readers need to know that it was sponsored. If you host giveaways or review products, you need to tell readers when you received the items for free. Put standards for sponsored posts and sources in your style guide.

Blogs give you space to stretch out and cover topics your readers care about. Email is another great place for that.

---

2 www.propublica.org/about/steal-our-stories/

3 www.ftc.gov/sites/default/files/attachments/press-releases/ftc-staff-revises-online-advertising-disclosure-guidelines/130312dotcomdisclosures.pdf

Email newsletters

Despite email's reputation, it's not just for selling things. Newsletter subscribers are a lot more engaged than most people who follow you on social media. They already care about what you have to say, which is why they asked for updates in the first place.

Since you're writing to a known group of loyal readers, you can be more casual and talk to them like friends sitting around your kitchen table. In some ways, writing an email is a lot like writing a letter. You're sending it to someone who will read it alongside notes from friends, family, and colleagues. It will wait until they're ready to read, instead of flowing by in a stream. Think about the kinds of things people want to read in that moment, and write to them where they are.

Another benefit of email is that there's a Reply button. Unlike a web page or blog post, people can reply privately. That's really meaningful. One-to-one replies are more intimate than public ones like blog comments (and they tend to be kinder). Make your newsletter more personal by reminding readers that they're welcome to respond.

Newsletter basics

Here are a few basics to keep in mind, no matter what kind of emails you send.

Think before you email

Email is cheap (or even free), so it's tempting to send all the time. Don't do that! It will annoy people, and they'll unsubscribe—or, worse—mark you as spam. Getting your frequency right takes some trial and error, but the best rule of thumb is to email only when you have something to say. Respect your readers' time. Make sure every note is useful, interesting, or otherwise deserving of the sacred space that is the inbox. You don't have to send an email newsletter every day or even every week.

If you send a newsletter called "Daily Words of Inspiration," then you're locked into daily emails. Otherwise, think about what makes sense for your readers. You can find out by asking them on your signup form, or monitoring your open, click, and unsubscribe rates.

Be courteous

Ask people for permission to email them (it's the law). Tell them what to expect and when to expect it. If you plan to start emailing more frequently, let your subscribers know ahead of time so they have a chance to think about it. If readers sign up for long-form articles about beer and get sale announcements about glassware, they're not going to be pleased. And of course, include a clear unsubscribe link in every email (that's also the law). There's no point in making it harder for people to leave when they already have one foot out the door.

Make subject lines specific

In an interview with *The Atlantic*, Stephen King said this about the opening line of a book: "An opening line should invite the reader to begin the story. It should say: Listen. Come in here. You want to know about this."[4] The same sentiment applies to an email subject line. It's an invitation to read on. Be descriptive and succinct.

Tell what's inside; don't sell what's inside. Let people know what you're writing about so they can decide whether or not to open your note. If you need help, almost any email service provider will let you quickly test subject lines to see what works best for your readers. Here are a few subject lines that tell what's inside:

> How to Know If You Have a Gluten Intolerance
> New Bruce Springsteen Record In Stock
> Banana Pudding Cupcakes and More New Flavors

Don't be a robot

In the From line, use your name or your company's name, instead of something like "noreply@rude.com." Your readers want to feel like these messages are coming from a real person, not an email robot. Signing off with your name or your team's name is a simple way to personalize it.

---

4 Joe Fassler, "Why Stephen King Spends 'Months and Even Years' Writing Opening Sentences, *The Atlantic*, July 23, 2013, www.theatlantic.com/entertainment/archive/2013/07/why-stephen-king-spends-months-and-even-years-writing-opening-sentences/278043/

Types of newsletters

Deciding what to send is the hard part. Here are some ideas that might work for you.

- There's nothing wrong with sending your community a good, old-fashioned **weekly or monthly newsletter**. We see this a lot with nonprofits who need to update their donors, board members, and volunteers regularly. Startups and growing businesses can show early adopters they care by writing about what they're working on.

- Publishers often send **roundups** of things they've posted and top articles for the week. If you publish a lot of content, you can treat your email newsletter like a **mini publication**. Grace Bonney of Design*Sponge (http://designsponge.com) highlights some of the week's top posts from her blog, rounds up other articles based on a theme, and adds new tidbits to each email.

- If you write for different publications, your readers might want a **digest** of recent work. Freelance writer Ann Friedman sends a newsletter called The Ann Friedman Weekly (http://annfriedman.com/weekly), where she shares articles she's written, what she's reading, and other things she finds interesting.

- Some writers use email to experiment with **long-form** writing. Whether you send content that's exclusive to your newsletter or articles you plan to polish and publish elsewhere, readers like being along for the ride.

- A fun way to reward your loyal readers is to send them **sneak peeks** of what's going on behind the scenes in your world. Send photos of your workspace, stories behind your products, or lessons from a recent project.

- Online sellers may want to send **short marketing emails**, like news about your products, special offers, and upcoming sales. We'll talk about marketing in the next chapter, but here, we'll just remind you not to fill up everyone's inbox with dry promotional messages.

Social Print Studio's community-building emails

Social Print Studio is a startup known for making Printstagram, an Instagram photo print shop. Their playful and aspirational voice comes through in all of their copy.

Social Print Studio's founder, Benjamin Lotan, writes a lot of the company's content himself. The studio's emails usually feature special offers or product announcements, but they're sprinkled with photos of the office cat, anecdotes about the team, and other personal details that make readers feel like they're part of Benjamin's inner circle. "It's a little overly personal, it's a little weird, and it's just me trying to be honest about our business," he says. Email is the perfect place for this level of friendliness, since people who subscribe to your newsletter have invited you in.

Benjamin knows that his business is still in the early stage, so he's focused on building a community of loyal fans. "Our goal for our email marketing is to try and get our customers and fans emotionally invested with us and to entertain them," he says. Blasting impersonal product announcements would turn some people off. But when readers receive funny notes from the founder of a company they love, the accompanying product announcements are a lot more pleasant.

Benjamin holds his company's content close to his heart and writes a portion of every email himself. "I write it myself because I don't trust anyone else to do it," he says. "This company is my baby. As we expand, it's like the company is growing into a willful adolescent, and I'm the dad picking it up at 11:00 p.m. on a weekend—or in this case at 4:00 a.m., just before our email blasts are scheduled to go out—and making sure it's still my baby."

Social media

For a lot of companies, "community" is a synonym for "social media." Don't fall into that trap. You may find a loyal community on Twitter, Facebook, Pinterest, or Instagram—and people will certainly find you through friends there—but building a community is about much more than tweeting, posting, and pinning.

Remember your goals. Choose the social media sites that make sense for you, and don't overextend yourself. A software company will do better on Twitter than Pinterest, but it makes sense for a food magazine to pin recipes and photos. Before signing up for every social site, consider the topics you cover, and the best way to share them.

Practice your style. Write in a conversational voice, and encourage replies. Since your word count may be limited, do a tone check to make sure you're not coming across as curt or unhelpful. Be yourself, and focus on posting interesting content instead of making a splash.

Participate. Social media shouldn't be a one-way street. People follow you so they can interact with you, not just so you can market at them. Customers may use these channels to ask you questions or react to your content. Respond to them. And if people need technical help, send them in the right direction.

Don't butt in. Some companies monitor Twitter and blogs for their brand name and interject into every conversation about them. That's not very becoming. If someone tags you with a question or a comment, jump right in and talk to that person. But if people are talking amongst themselves, don't interrupt them.

As you share your content on social sites, remember to show your human side and think about how to build bridges with new readers.

Design Mom's growing community

Gabrielle Blair started a blog called Design Mom in 2007, to write about "where design and motherhood intersect." At the time, she was an art director in New York with five kids, and her peers were asking her for advice about things like baby products, birthday parties, and parenting in general. Since then, her blog has grown into a business with readers all over the world. She also cofounded an annual conference for bloggers called Altitude Summit, and works with photographers, advertisers, and other writers. A lot has changed, but Blair still writes about parenting through a design lens.

She's made some adjustments over time to accommodate the growth of her blog, and she listens closely to feedback from her community. Last year, she brought on a handful of contributors to write posts for Design Mom. They were great writers and longtime readers, but Blair's community didn't love the change. "Although I was still writing every day in 2013, I was getting feedback from readers that they wanted to hear more from me," she says. She still hires out for some of the photography and DIY posts on her site, but she's gone back to writing most of the content herself.

Blair says the best way to connect with readers on a personal level is to write from an honest place. "For me, it's all about writing posts that reflect what's happening in my life right then," she says. "If I'm struggling, I tell my readers so. If I'm passionate about something new in my life, I share it." She also listens hard and sets aside time to respond to comments from readers. Reading their responses and having conversations with them helps her gauge what matters to them.

Blair knows that she can't be a part of every single conversation that happens on her website, so she encourages her community members to connect with one another. "I want Design Mom to be a place where women from all walks of life feel comfortable sharing their experiences—and those experiences vary widely and are often in direct contrast with one another. So I've worked hard to create a really good commenting culture on Design Mom," she says. "No matter how controversial the topic—taxidermy, how many children you should have, plastic surgery—readers can share their experiences without fear of facing trolls or being belittled. I can't emphasize enough how important that has been."

Keep in touch

When your readership grows or your products take off, you'll have your community to thank. Remember those people, no matter how big your company becomes or how busy you get. Work hard to keep them happy. Stay in touch by replying to their posts, comments, and emails. Talk to them after events and ask them questions. Let them ask you questions, too. If you hear similar questions over and over, think about making a list of common questions and answers to help readers learn more about you. Turn that into a post and link to it in relevant places.

Look for ways to give your writing a human touch. If you sell products, personalize your receipts and return instructions. People are probably excited to receive their packages, so that's a good time to make an impression. If you work with clients, write thank-you notes on your own stationery. If you send email newsletters, offer a discount or surprise gift to thank your subscribers. Remember the little things, too, like signing your name at the end of your emails and thanking people for reaching out.

Ask for feedback

Ask your community what they want to hear from you. Request feedback casually when you meet people at events, or email readers you know. You may want to send out a simple survey through a service like SurveyMonkey or Survs. Think about exactly what you want to learn from your readers. Write a few clear questions, and keep it brief.

Avoid leading or biased questions:

> Are you enjoying our new and improved website design?

Instead, keep it neutral:

> We recently changed how books are sorted on our website. What do you think of the new layout?

Whether you send surveys or informal emails, or talk to people in your daily life, get in the habit of asking for feedback. It's a simple way to stay close to the heart of your community and improve your writing. Your readers will be happy to tell you about what they like, what they don't like, and what else they want to know.

Chapter Eight

SELL IT WITHOUT SELLING OUT

THINK ABOUT YOUR FAVORITE COMPANIES. What do they sell? What do you like about them so much? Now think about all the ways they communicate with you. Maybe you've been to their websites or seen their advertising campaigns. Or maybe you subscribe to their newsletters or follow them on social media sites. Chances are, they write in a way that's consistent, friendly, and easy to understand. That's part of why you love them and keep coming back.

Some people cringe at the idea of marketing. Many companies say and do obnoxious things to sell their products. But marketing doesn't have to spin the truth, and it doesn't have to be smarmy. If you're uncomfortable with the idea of selling, read on. We'll help you write to sell without those cringe-inducing moments.

Helping people and making them happy is the best kind of marketing you can do. Once you have a community, you can even count on the people in it to do some of your marketing for you. People who love you and your products will tell their friends. So before you spend a bunch of time and money on marketing materials, make sure your current readers and customers are happy. Give them good, clear information that they'll want to pass around. If you're doing it right, they'll spread the love.

Of course, your customers can't do *all* the marketing for you. As a writer, part of your job is to tell people what you're selling and persuade them to take the next step: buy a product, use a service, read an article, or hire you. In this chapter, we'll talk about:

- Principles of effective marketing copy
- How to write marketing messages for your company
- Developing bios, taglines, landing pages, product descriptions, and more

These concepts and examples will show you how to write useful copy that helps you sell without selling out.

We're all in marketing

As David Packard famously said, "Marketing is too important to be left to the marketing department." Everyone who writes for the web needs to understand the importance of marketing. Whether or not you're on a marketing team, you're working on something that people are buying, using, or reading. We all have something to sell. If you're a blogger, you may be building up your name and selling yourself. If you provide a service, you're selling your expertise and experience. And if you sell products, a huge part of building a customer base is being able to introduce what you make in a friendly way.

Content is almost always an advertisement—even when it's not intended to be.

In his book *To Sell Is Human*, Daniel Pink says:

> To sell well is to convince someone else to part with resources—not to deprive that person, but to leave him better off in the end. That is also what, say, a good algebra teacher does. At the beginning of a term, students don't know much about the subject. But the teacher works to convince his class to part with

resources—time, attention, effort—and if they do, they will be better off when the term ends than they were when it began.[1]

Whether you're trying to get people to buy your product, read your blog, or trust your brand, tell them why they'll be better off for doing it. That's your spark.

Tell your story

A good story helps you get people's attention. Like the rest of your marketing, stories should teach people something new or inspire them to get involved. It's hard to predict what will resonate with people, so try practicing your story on a friend. Think about what makes *you* excited about what you sell.

Your story could be about how you got started or why you do what you do. The husband-and-wife team behind Quinn Popcorn puts their story right on every box:

> When our son Quinn was born we set out on a mission to clean up our favorite childhood snack. It took years, but the proof that it's possible is in your hands.

That little piece of copy slows you down for a second when you're about to tear into a bag of popcorn. It's a thoughtful way to share the company's history at an unexpected moment. The website features photos of the family and blog posts about new flavors, package design, and the struggles of running a startup food company. They market their story and their values as much as the popcorn itself. And along the way, they help people discover that popcorn can—and should—be better. They focus on the quality of their products, not just on the box, but in almost all of their marketing copy, using phrases like "farm-to-bag," "cleaning up microwave popcorn," and "microwave popcorn reinvented."

---

1 Daniel H. Pink, *To Sell Is Human: The Surprising Truth about Moving Others* (New York: Riverhead Books, 2013), 38.

If you have an interesting story that touches every aspect of your business, then by all means, share it with your readers. Focus on why your work matters. If you don't have a particularly interesting story, that's okay too. Just leave it out of your marketing copy and focus on the people you're helping instead.

Interestingness of your story aside, don't get carried away writing a lengthy About page. Most people won't take the time to read paragraphs and paragraphs about your team or company history.

Marketing principles

Your marketing copy should be true to your company's spirit. You can be enthusiastic, as long as it sounds like something you'd say. Here are some basic principles to help you keep it real.

Clarity above all

Avoid dramatic metaphors and flowery language. Instead, choose words that people will understand and stick with short, conversational sentences. Stay away from jargon, too. If you sell jewelry, call it jewelry, not "wearable art." If you sell office supplies, call them office supplies, not "corporate solutions." It's more important to be clear than unique.

Focus on the benefits

Tell people exactly how you can help them, and focus on your actual strengths. Listen to what your customers say about why they use your products, instead of talking about why *you* think they do. Don't call yourself the best, the fastest, or the most powerful. That's not usually true, for starters—we can't all be the best. But more importantly, people see right through that kind of language. You'll earn trust by being honest and making good on your promises.

Watch your adverbs and modifiers, because they can get in the way of more important words. Calling an announcement "incredibly exciting"

Kristina Halvorson's advice to marketers

Kristina Halvorson is the CEO of Brain Traffic, founder of Confab Events, and coauthor of *Content Strategy for the Web*. She speaks about the role of marketing in the larger context of a company's content, and advises her clients on copywriting and marketing strategy.

Kristina says a lot of marketing teams are so busy rushing to create the latest and greatest social media campaign that they lose sight of their customers' needs. "I want marketers to stop for a minute, take a breath, and talk to their customers—not about what they like, necessarily, but what they need. And, as marketers, we need to be brave and really hear what our customers are saying," she says. "If you're selling laundry detergent, it's unlikely your customers will care about your super awesome YouTube videos if your product still can't get grass stains out of their kids' jeans."

Kristina emphasizes the importance of setting long-term goals: "I feel like I spend a lot of my time talking people out of *more* content and into *less* content. Marketers tend to measure short-term activities and outcomes—how did this campaign perform, what's our email click-through rate, how many likes do we have on Facebook, and so on. I believe that true marketing content is content that *meets our customers' needs* at every point in the buying lifecycle, including post-purchase." She adds that marketers should consider technical and support content every bit as important as pre-purchase content, and ensure that everything they write supports the company's goals and meets the readers' needs.

---

doesn't, in fact, make it incredibly exciting. Instead, say what *does* make it exciting. Maybe you're talking about something that solves a real problem, saves money, is good for the environment, helps people get their work done, teaches them a new skill, or helps them relax.

Make it useful

Some companies still believe that marketing is about reach and visibility. They think that if they just get their name in front of as many eyeballs as possible, people are sure to buy in. The problem with this approach is that when you try to speak to everyone, you usually end up speaking loudly to no one in particular.

Instead of marketing into a megaphone, figure out who you want to talk to first. Do your research, and let conversations with real customers guide your decisions. Give your primary and secondary audiences good information that's relevant and interesting. Don't worry about the people you're *not* trying to do business with.

Think about the last time you had a good shopping or dining experience. Maybe your server made you feel special and got everything just right. Or maybe the sales associate made your day by answering your questions without trying to upsell you. Effective marketing is saying the right thing to the right people at the right time. It doesn't feel like a tired sales pitch or an over-the-top attention-getter. It doesn't disrespect or manipulate the reader. It's there to sell, but it's helpful and down-to-earth too.

Message matters

Think about your company's defining characteristics. How do your products improve people's lives? What ideas do you want readers to take away from your site? These are your marketing messages. They tell people how you're different, and why they should care about your company.

Marketing messages help you decide which points to cover, and often thread different content types together with similar ideas.

We recommend writing a primary message and a few secondary messages. For example, here's what Shortstack Books' primary message might be:

> Shortstack Books is a fun place where kids can find new books to read.

This message should come through in all of Shortstack's content. It's the most important thing to convey in the copy.

Secondary messages speak to more specific needs, or a subset of your customers. In *The Elements of Content Strategy*, Erin Kissane divides these messages into three categories: rational, emotional, and reputation-based.[2] Let's look at possible secondary messages for Shortstack.

Rational messages

These messages appeal to the reader's rational mind. Focus on practical, everyday needs, like solving a problem, or saving time and money. Here are two copy examples with those messages:

> We handpick every book so you don't have to.

> Free shipping on orders over $25.

You could also promise to entertain your readers or teach them something new, like so:

> We run in-store events where kids can meet their favorite authors.

> Parents can enjoy spending time at our shop while their kids explore.

Set yourself apart by telling people *how* you're different. Maybe you sell a specific genre or accept trade-ins. These facts are useful for readers.

Emotional messages

Emotional messages appeal to people's feelings, hopes, and dreams. They're more aspirational, and show your softer side.

Reading is fun, so you could spell that out:

> Books are fun to read—and our store is full of adventures.

---

2 Erin Kissane, *The Elements of Content Strategy* (New York: A Book Apart, 2011), 29.

Say what you'll do to make readers happy, satisfy their curiosity, or brighten their day.

> Reading is a great way to relax in the evenings and spend time with your kids before you tuck them in.

> Find books for anything you're curious about.

If you know your readers are passionate about something, you can appeal to that too.

Reputation-based messages

You can also talk about your reputation. Some people want solid proof that they're making a good choice. If you have a presence on social media sites like Facebook and Yelp, include those recommendations. Here's an example for a small business:

> We have 20 five-star reviews on Yelp.

Whatever combination of messages you choose, put them in writing and use them to get your point across. People will start to associate those messages with your company. You may need to change your messages as your company grows. Revisit them regularly to be sure they match up with your strengths.

Introduce yourself

Now that you've articulated what's special about you, start pulling your marketing messages into your copy. Your bio is a great place to begin.

Bios

Don't you just hate writing bios? We hear you. Writing about yourself is a lot of pressure. But everyone needs a bio, and being able to write one is an important skill to have. We recommend writing at least two versions of your bio: a long one and a short one. No matter what kind of business you're in, you'll need bios of different lengths for different contexts. For instance, you may want a longer version for your About page, and a short one for social media profiles, event pages, and press releases.

Write your long bio first. It doesn't need to be exhaustive—keep it to four or five sentences. Tell people what you do, using familiar terms, and then tell them why you do it.

First, say exactly what it is that you do. Here are some prompts to get you started:

> I'm a _____ .
>
> We're a _____ company.
>
> That means we _____ .
>
> We help people _____ .
>
> My day-to-day looks like _____ .

Then say why you do it. This part can be clever, playful, or inspirational, if that's your style.

> Because I love _____ .
>
> Because people need _____ .
>
> We believe _____ .
>
> I care about _____ .

Using that simple structure, here's what Shortstack's bio might look like:

> Shortstack is a children's bookstore in Pittsburgh. We sell a wide selection of handpicked books, and we hold summer camps and classes that encourage kids to love reading. We also offer books for grown-ups to enjoy while their kids explore. We believe in the power of reading.

Your long bio can include details about the size of your company, your clients, recent projects, features, or your website. You may also want to include specific information for the press, investors, or clients. Add those elements after you get the main point across, and close with a memorable line.

Now, let's take the most important parts of the bio and make a short version. Your short bio should say what you do in one or two sentences.

> Shortstack is a children's bookstore in Pittsburgh. We offer a handpicked selection of books and host summer reading camps.

If you're a freelancer, write a pitch so you don't get tongue tied when a potential client asks what you do. Use a similar approach: explain what you do, but instead of saying why you do it, say what you're hoping to achieve. Here's what a freelance designer's pitch could look like:

> I'm a freelance designer. I help clients create beautiful websites, mobile apps, and marketing campaigns. I'd love to chat about the projects you're working on.

Taglines

You've heard the classic taglines, like "Got Milk?" "Just Do It," and "Don't Leave Home Without It." These short, catchy slogans usually appear below a company logo or at the end of an advertisement. Taglines don't always fit on a website, so some companies don't use them. They're totally optional, but they can be fun to play around with.

Taglines set the tone for the rest of your marketing. If you publish content in different places, like radio, TV, billboards, and the web, taglines can make your company more memorable. When you come up with one you like, picture it in different contexts. Taglines have to read well *and* sound good when they're said out loud. Here are a few examples:

Seamless (food delivery):

> Your food is here.

Airbnb (vacation rentals):

> Find a place to stay.

SoundCloud (music and audio community):

> Hear the world's sounds.

Each of these taglines tells you what to expect in a few words.

If you decide to write a tagline, start by brainstorming. Think about how you want people to feel about your brand. Jot down familiar words and phrases that align with your mission and your main marketing message. Your tagline should be pithy and memorable, and it should sound like something you'd say out loud. Cut any words that are vague or overly specific, and leave a little room for the imagination.

Campaign taglines

Some companies write taglines for specific campaigns or product launches. Like a brand tagline, a campaign tagline appears in more than one place. It usually has an expiration date or is tied to a launch. Apple does this all the time. When they launch a new product, they use the tagline everywhere: on their product page, signage, billboards, and TV ads. Here are some examples:

> iPad: What will your verse be?
> iPhone 5c: For the colorful.
> iMac: Performance and design. Taken right to the edge.

All of these taglines touch on what's special about the product. The iPad one is more aspirational, while the iPhone one says what's different about the 5c (the colors). The iMac one tells you more directly what you're getting.

A note about branding and capitalization

Some companies capitalize terms in taglines and marketing to try to claim them as trademarks. This can be useful for software companies who want to distinguish themselves from competitors or claim specific words, like *Pin*, *Tweet*, or *News Feed*. But people tend to lowercase common words and phrases—even if you ask them not to—so think twice before replacing a familiar word with a Branded Term. Along those lines, don't try to trademark every word in your tagline. When in doubt, ask yourself if your branding is important enough to risk distracting or confusing people.

Headlines

Headlines are great for highlighting a particular message or summarizing a page on a marketing website. Think of it as your shining moment to make an entrance. Headlines can be playful, but they should also be tangible. Here are two prompts to help you write effective marketing headlines.

Cut to the verbs. Answer this question in a complete sentence: What do you want people to do with your website? Here are two examples for Shortstack:

> We want to help people find children's books they love.

> We want people to sign up for our in-store events and summer camps.

Next, cut straight to the active verbs.

> ~~We want to help people~~ find the best children's books.

> ~~We want people to~~ sign up for our in-store events and summer camps.

That right there could be your headline, or at least a good starting point.

Take charge. Pretend for a moment that you're in command of the universe. What do you want people to do? Tell them in a clear, powerful voice. Here are some examples:

> Read books every day.
> Find something new to read.
> Stop by tomorrow to save 30 percent on picture books.

Be direct, but nice. It'll make your sentences shorter and stronger.

Now let's work through other content types for your homepage or marketing pages.

Answer questions and sell it

After introducing yourself, highlight the most important details. You don't need to explain the ins-and-outs of every part of your website on the homepage. Give people an overview, and then point them in the right direction. Expect them to skim and scan—so keep the content short and focused.

Address real-world questions: what you're selling, who it's for, what it *actually* does, why it matters, how it works, and where to get it. Use plain language. If you have to make up fancy terms or phrases, you may be veering into fantasyland. Help your reader understand how you're different from the competition, without using words like "better" and "best." Make a list of questions you want to answer, and check them off once you have a draft.

Product and event descriptions

Short descriptions are useful for explaining products, features, and events. Maybe you teach classes or give talks locally. Or maybe you sell apps or handmade goods. Use this brief format to tell people what they're getting for their time, money, or attention.

First things first

Put the most important details at the top. What will encourage the reader to take the next step or make a purchase? Focus on clarity over cleverness.

Come up with a system for how you describe things. If you're selling products, include the price, product name, color, size, materials, and manufacturer. If you're writing about an event, include the date, time, location, and details like whether food will be provided. Shortstack Books could include titles, author and publisher names, imprint details, pricing, and notes on a book's length and condition. Some sites give you predefined fields for product details—so you may be able to skip them in the copy itself.

Make it a good read

Use active verbs in product descriptions. Tell customers what needs you're meeting and how. If you're selling something, spell out any specific features or benefits. If you're advertising an event, tell people what to expect throughout the day. You could also include reviews from customers or press mentions. If you know something special about this item, say so in a friendly way.

Here's a sample description for the book *Stay Up Late* on Shortstack's website:

> *Stay Up Late* features full-color illustrations of the classic hit song by the Talking Heads. This book is wrapped in an acid-free jacket and has a reinforced binding.

Limit each sentence to one idea. For longer descriptions, rearrange your sentences into a short list of bullet points.

Tell them how you really feel

Another way to make things more personal is to try out the product and give your honest opinion. Storq sells maternity essentials online for moms-to-be. Along with their clothing line, the shop features body and beauty products from other manufacturers, tested by the Storq staff. Each product description is short, conversational, and written in the company's voice. Here's the introduction for a shampoo:

> You know those natural shampoos that instantly strip your hair of all its moisture so it feels like straw? Hate those.

Storq shows their human side by talking to their readers as friends.

Calls to action

Sometimes you have to tell people exactly what to do. Calls to action are links or button labels that ask the reader to take the next step.

Start by making a list of the actions people can take on your site. Here are some common examples:

Read more	Sign up
See all results	Check out now
Learn more	Add a comment
Add to cart	

Look at your list and ask yourself what you *really* want the reader to do. Those are the ones you'll want to test and refine.

A word or three

Limit calls to action to five words or less. Start with an active verb. Use the second-person voice, and avoid referencing yourself. In some cases, you may want to include *now* at the end of the phrase to create a sense of urgency. In others, that may sound too demanding—or it may not make a difference at all.

Say what's next

Tell readers what's on the next page so they know exactly what to expect. Here are a few examples we could try on the Shortstack site:

Complete your purchase	Find a great gift
Visit the shop	Meet the shop owners
Browse the selection	Join this event
See the collection	

As always, clarity comes first. Don't be too clever. With buttons, you should use standard language that people are used to seeing. For example, if you're trying to get people to sign up for something, your button should say exactly that: Sign up.

Customer stories

One way to bolster your arguments is to have someone back you up in their own words. Customer stories and testimonials show off your strengths without sounding like you're bragging. Here are three examples:

- Tell readers how you helped a client or customer. **Case studies** can take on various forms: blog posts, video interviews, email newsletters, or homepage spotlights. Say what happened, and what made the project interesting, without exaggerating. If something was difficult, say that too. Your readers might relate. Include metrics if you have them.

- You can also tell stories **from your community**. Clothing retailers like Everlane (http://everlane.com) and Of a Kind (http://ofakind.com) highlight the people who make their clothing and accessories. That's a better read than stories about people wearing clothes.

- **Testimonials** are another way to share praise from customers. These brief quotes are useful for product companies and freelancers. Ask happy customers for a brief recommendation. Pull out the best part, add a photo, link to their website, and you're all set.

Feature topics that make sense for your readers, and focus on positive changes.

Refine the copy

Once you have a rough draft of your marketing copy, pull it all together in the order you want people to read it. Work through a few full-page drafts to see that everything reads well and sounds like you. Make sure your copy is consistent, double-checking for keywords and capitalization in headlines. If you gathered up ratings, reviews, or testimonials, sprinkle those in where they count. Focus on the essentials.

This stuff takes time. You won't start brainstorming today and finalize your marketing messages tomorrow. The first draft of your bio will probably make you cringe, but you've got it on paper, and you'll refine it from there. Take the time to learn what works for you and your customers. If you test your copy, test responsibly. Don't get carried away with the numbers when your primary concern should be the words. Your website is the first experience most people will have with your company, so make it count.

Chapter Nine

TOUCHY SUBJECTS

IMAGINE YOU'RE OUT getting the mail, and someone pulls over to ask you for directions. They're flushed and seem to be in a hurry. How would you respond? You'd probably answer quickly, getting right to the point and skipping any introductions or small talk. That's because you don't know where that person is trying to go or why. When you're giving information in a situation like this, it's especially important to be calm, clear, and helpful.

You don't know what's going on in your readers' lives. You don't know their worries and concerns. But you do know the circumstances you're creating for them, and you can write in a way that makes those moments a little easier.

In this chapter, we'll talk about:

- Writing error messages, alerts, and help documents
- Apologizing with grace
- Working with lawyers on terms and policies

These are important moments to show readers that you care about their feelings.

Writing with empathy

Readers have their own opinions, preferences, values, and touchy subjects. They bring all of that with them when they visit your website. So no matter what you're writing, it's important to use inclusive language and think about your timing.

Some industries are sensitive by nature. For example, if you write for a healthcare organization, your readers may be scared, hurting, or facing a financial burden. Banks have to be careful for some of the same reasons: they're handling money and personal information—and people don't trust them.[1] Fundraising is also tricky. Asking for money is never easy, and being asked for money isn't so fun, either. If you're working in these industries, everything you write carries extra weight.

Let's look at some touchy subjects that may come across your desk. By now, you should have a list of content types you work on. Review it with your readers in mind, and identify any that you'd consider sensitive or urgent subjects. These could include:

- Error messages, like credit card declines
- Downtime notifications
- Support documentation or help content
- Customer service emails and chats
- Terms of service and legal policies
- Community guidelines

Now, think about why those subjects are sensitive. What situations are your readers in when they see the content? Your tone can make a big difference here.

---

1 Edelman, "Trust in U.S. Financial Services Still Low Despite Economic, Market Gains," March 13, 2012, http://trust.edelman.com/slides/trust-in-u-s-financial-services-still-low-despite-economic-market-gains/.

Under pressure

When you're writing for sensitive situations, keep these guidelines in mind:

Act quickly. Whether you're telling customers that their data was compromised, announcing changes to your privacy policy, or giving someone an official warning, it's important to respond quickly. Readers want to know what's going on right away.

Get to the point. Don't waste anyone's time with an introduction like "We regret to inform you…" That will get on your readers' nerves and increase their anxiety. Say as little as you can while being clear, kind, and direct. If you're sending an email about changes to your privacy policy, put those words right in the subject line, instead of something general like "An Important Update."

Stay calm. Don't panic. Leave out the exclamation marks. Avoid using words like *alert, immediately,* and *urgent* unless they're absolutely necessary. Write calmly so people can focus on your message.

Don't try to lighten the mood. If you try to distract people with a clever joke or marketing spiel, they'll see right through it. A sensitive situation isn't the place to inject your personality.

Be honest. You won't always be able to tell readers everything that's going on, but be as transparent as possible. If you're announcing a delay, include a timeline or estimate. If you were running late to dinner at a friend's house, you probably wouldn't say, "Hello, I'm going to be late." Instead, you'd be more specific and say something like, "In traffic, running about 10 minutes late." Your readers deserve that same level of courtesy.

If you need someone to take another step like change a password or agree to a new policy, then spell that out and say how to do it. And if you're writing about a situation that's still developing, offer to update your readers as more information unfolds.

When to stay out of it

Unless it relates to your business, stay away from polarizing topics like religion and political commentary. And if you write blog posts or social media updates, be aware of what's happening in the news so your content doesn't come off as insensitive. When there's a crisis going on, like a hurricane or a shooting, people look to Twitter for news. During unrelated emergencies, keep quiet and turn off any auto-tweets or scheduled posts. We don't even recommend saying things like "Our thoughts go out to the people affected," especially if you're not helping to resolve the situation. Some companies feel like they need to get a word in no matter the circumstances, but the most respectful thing to do is avoid cluttering people's news feeds with unnecessary information.

Sensitive situations

In Chapter 6: Watch Your Tone, we talked about how it can be helpful to think of your messages in terms of good news and bad news. Most sensitive content types fall under the category of bad news.

Urgent topics

If something goes wrong, you may have to be the bearer of bad news. Here are a few situations to prepare for in advance.

Error messages

Error messages can include everything from "This post is no longer available" to "Your credit card has been declined." It's a message for when something goes wrong, possibly on your end. Error messages don't need to be overly apologetic, since they're usually system-related and not a personal mistake or miscommunication. They do need to be kind, though, because credit card declines and similar messages are potentially embarrassing. Let people know what went wrong, but also tell them what they should do next: refresh the page, fill in a blank field, or come back in a few minutes. And don't blame the reader with a message like "You followed a bad link."

Emergencies

Emergencies include catastrophes or data breaches that could compromise a server and keep employees from making it to work. If something causes your website to go down, delays service or order fulfillment, or limits customer service, then tell your customers immediately. Give them as much detail as possible about what's happening. But if data is involved, be careful not to share information that could create a security threat. Let your customers know that you're doing everything you can, and keep them updated.

Use a sympathetic and helpful tone, and apologize if it's appropriate. (We'll talk about apologies in detail later in this chapter.) Share your contact information, so people can reach out with any questions or concerns. This will give them a sense of security when they're feeling uneasy.

When Squarespace lost power during Hurricane Sandy in 2012, their founder and CEO Anthony Casalena sent a couple of emails to customers. The company's headquarters were running on a generator when the power first went out, so there was time to warn people. The first email's subject line was direct: "Downtime due to Hurricane Sandy." It explained what had happened and when the company expected the service to be disrupted, down to the hour. It went on to reassure customers: "Be assured that while this will impact our availability, there is no chance of data loss or any other permanent effects. We have simply run out of power, backup power, and cannot access our fuel in a flooded basement." Squarespace didn't apologize, because the situation wasn't the company's fault. Instead, the email calmly thanked readers for understanding.

About a week later, they sent another update with some good news: no customers had experienced downtime during the storm. The email explained that the headquarters had a working pump system, enough fuel, and a generator for backup. It also said they were working on a more efficient system in case of another emergency. Meanwhile, the company updated its Status page so customers could see what was happening with the servers. Between the prompt emails and the Status page, Squarespace left no questions unanswered.

Prepare for the worst

If you can predict some of the urgent or sensitive situations that may come up, write a few templates for those messages. That way, when you have to send an email or post a tweet about unexpected downtime, you can update your template to fit the situation and publish it right away.

Consider the worst-case scenarios for your business. What would you do if there were an earthquake or data theft? If you depend on Etsy or Shopify to sell your products, how you would communicate if that service went down? The notification in these circumstances might surprise your customers and cause them anxiety. Write to them with those feelings in mind. And if you're planning for downtime or know that one of your service providers is, warn customers ahead of time.

You can also make an emergency contact list. Think of all the people you depend on to keep your business running. Who would you call if your website went down? What about your payment system or warehouse team, if you sell physical goods? Include a mix of subject-matter experts in case you need quick answers, and who to contact for late-night publishing approval, especially if you need to run something by a director or legal counsel first. Having a list like this can also help other writers when you're out of the office.

Less urgent situations

Some sensitive content types—like help documents, chat messages, and unsubscribe confirmations—aren't necessarily bad news, but a considerate tone is important for them too. Even though it's not a drop-everything emergency, the same principles apply.

Help documents and FAQs

If your customers are reading help documents, knowledge base articles, or tutorials on your site, it's safe to assume that they're troubleshooting.

Maybe they need to figure out how to complete a task, or your service isn't working for them and they're looking for help. If you rub them the wrong way now, they might lose trust in you. If you help them find what they're looking for and make the process painless, they might come out of the experience more loyal than before.

Help documents should be comprehensive and clear without overwhelming your customers or insulting their intelligence. They should be as useful as a great support rep would be in person. Doing this is harder than it seems. Walk people through the steps, one at a time, and don't assume that they know how to do certain things. Remember that you're an expert, but they aren't. If you're telling them to click a button, name the button. Include screenshots or illustrations where possible, and provide links to related documents when it makes sense. Use an encouraging and positive tone, but avoid overly friendly or flowery language.

Here's an example of a simple and to-the-point help article from Harvest, an invoicing and time-tracking software company.[2]

How to Create an Invoice Step-by-Step
Administrators can create invoices for all clients. Project managers can create invoices for projects they manage if they have been given permission to create invoices under **Manage > People**.

Based on Project Hours and Expenses
1. Go to **Invoices > Overview**.

2. Click **Create Invoice**, and pick your client.

3. To pull in hours from your timesheet, choose to invoice **Based on project hours and expenses**, and click **Next Step**. Remember, **tasks must be checked as billable** on your project (under **Manage > Projects**) in order to be pulled into an invoice.

4. Fill out the **Create Invoice** page, and click **Create Invoice**.

---

2 www.getharvest.com/help/invoices-and-estimates/get-started/how-to-create-an-invoice

5. You'll see a draft of the invoice. You can add a subject, due date, taxes, customize the orders of the rows on your invoice, and more.

6. Click **Save Invoice**. You can send your invoice right away, or save a draft and send it later.

You can tell that the Harvest team checked their work carefully. The title is clear, and they specify which tabs and buttons to click in bold text.

Contact pages are similar. Sometimes people will contact you to tell you how wonderful you are. But most of the time, customers visit that page because they have a problem or a specific question. That's why these types of pages should be concise and get right to the point.

Canned responses

Canned (or pre-written) responses are useful for companies that provide support over chat or email. The goal is to write them in a fresh way, so there's no whiff of that canned smell. If you've ever chatted with your bank or your cable company, you've probably received canned responses. If you're a blogger or small business owner and you get recurring questions from readers, canned responses may be useful for you too. On a smaller scale, you could even think of an out-of-office message as a canned response.

Canned responses are similar to help documents in that you want to be brief, straightforward, and friendly. But instead of writing out a procedure, you can link people to useful articles to keep the messages short and sweet.

Make the writing conversational. Here's a bad example of a customer service chat with Time Warner to avoid recreating:

Customer: I need to reset my router's login information.

Agent: Thank you for sharing the information. I completely understand your concern. I will be glad to assist you with that... Please give me a moment to review your account so I can provide the best possible solution to you.

Customer: Sure, thank you.

Agent: I appreciate your time and patience. I would like to inform you that I will have to transfer this chat to our higher level of support to assist you further with your concern and resolve your issue. Please wait while the problem is escalated to another analyst...

Yikes. Don't be so formal that you waste people's time. Bring your voice in here, too. And if you're combining several canned responses, read through them as a whole before sending them off—and cut anything that's not helpful. You don't want to sound like a robot, especially when someone's troubleshooting a problem.

Unsubscribe confirmations

If you send email newsletters, spend some time on your unsubscribe flow. When people decide to unsubscribe from a newsletter, they usually have to check a box or click a button to confirm their decision. After that, they're sent to another screen that says they were, in fact, removed from the list. This can be a turning point for readers, where the right tone of voice can go a long way. These pages often have generic, automatically generated copy that says something like "You have been unsubscribed from this newsletter." If you remain neutral, you probably won't make anyone mad.

But why be neutral when you can make people smile? That's what Barack Obama's team did when he was running for reelection in 2012. The unsubscribe confirmation said this:

"I'm voting for the President in 2012—I just get too many emails."

That's what a lot of folks who end up on this page say. Here's why we think you should stick around: If you want to see the President re-elected in 2012, you should stay looped in on the efforts to make it happen.

Just looking to get fewer emails? We can send you campaign updates only once a week or so. Be sure to select your preferred frequency option below.

This message acknowledged people's feelings and even gave them an option to stay on the list with fewer emails. The tone was understanding but persuasive, and it probably convinced a lot of subscribers to stick around.

Meanwhile, his opponent's unsubscribe message said this:

> Thank you! You have been unsubscribed from this publication.

When people say they don't want to hear from you again, it's probably not a good idea to thank them emphatically. This message lacks empathy and comes off as tone-deaf.

Even if you don't give readers an option to change the frequency of emails, you can still offer them other ways to keep in touch. Photojojo, a company that sells photography-related products online, has a lighthearted tone and a goofy sense of humor. A customer who unsubscribes receives the following message: "We're sorry to see you go." After the customer confirms, this message appears: "OK, so email wasn't for us. But HEY there's lotsa ways to stay in touch," accompanied by links to their social media pages. This friendly approach leaves the reader with happy feelings about the brand.

An unsubscribe confirmation is an example of an often overlooked moment that deserves your attention.

A graceful apology

Some companies seem to apologize every single day (airlines, anyone?). Others only have to apologize when something big happens, like a data breach or a major outage. Apologizing is tricky. Here are some things to keep in mind when saying you're sorry.

Own it

If you travel regularly, then you've probably had a delayed flight. Sometimes you don't find out your flight is delayed until you're at the gate. And then the corporate non-apology comes over the intercom: "Our apologies for any inconvenience this may have caused." That's not enough. "We apologize" is better than "our apologies" because it's an action, and "we're sorry" is better than both because it sounds more human and genuine. However you phrase it, take responsibility.

When *The Atlantic* published an advertisement for Scientology that looked a little too much like editorial content in 2013, it caused an uproar. *The Atlantic* pulled the article and issued an official apology. The first sentence was: "We screwed up." They went on to say that the company was figuring out guidelines and policies for sponsored content. The apology ended with this humble signoff:

> We remain committed to and enthusiastic about innovation in digital advertising, but acknowledge—sheepishly—that we got ahead of ourselves. We are sorry, and we're working very hard to put things right.

Their honesty and willingness to admit the error helped them earn back readers' trust. We've all done things we regret, and we know what it's like to be embarrassed about it. This apology came across as considered and sincere.

Say what you're sorry for

Let's go back to the classic non-apology: "Our apologies for any inconvenience this may have caused." Telling people you regret "any inconvenience" isn't going to make them feel like you care one bit. In the case of a flight delay, "We're sorry for the delay" or "We're sorry for the frustration" would be better. Remember the worst-case scenario. One of those people sitting at the gate could be missing a family reunion or a job interview because the flight is late. That's much more than an "inconvenience." If people feel like you understand what you did wrong and how it affected them, they're more likely to believe that you won't let it happen again.

Say what happens next

Don't forget to tell readers what you're going to do next or what they should expect. This is especially important in the case of an outage, data breach, or delay. If you can offer something to make it up to them, spell that out. If you're writing to say you're sorry about unexpected downtime, explain that you're working to fix it. Let people know that you'll send another notification when things are back to normal. That gives them a sense of security. Apologies are stressful, but you can lessen the stress by acting quickly, communicating calmly, and getting right to the point.

Let's move on to another touchy subject we all have to deal with: legal and privacy-related content.

Legal writing

Readers often skip over contracts, terms, and policies—but writing them doesn't have to be dull work. In fact, your terms are a huge part of how you build relationships with customers. Think of them like an initial meeting with a client. You want to be clear and open about what you'll do for each other. You also want to show that you intend to have a balanced and long-term relationship.

You'll work with lawyers on terms, privacy messages, disclosures, community guidelines, contracts, and user agreements. These are the places where you put your promises into writing. For example, you may need to share a link to your return policy in a checkout flow or ask people to accept your data use policy when they create an account. Or you may want people to know what happens when they connect your app to Facebook. These are all potentially sticky situations where customers need to understand what they're agreeing to. By choosing to use your site, people are often accepting a legally binding contract. So this is serious business.

Most terms are written poorly. The language is confusing and full of Latin phrases that people don't understand. The agreements themselves are long and hard to read, which is bad news for you and your readers, because you need to be clear about your policies. That wall of all-caps, angry-looking text can make people wonder what's hiding behind it. The good news is that the bar is so low with legal content that you can stand out by making your terms friendly and easy to read. Let's look at how to do that by working closely with your lawyer.

Teaming up on terms

The first thing to remember is that your legal team acts on behalf of your company and its interests—which may or may not include your readers' interests. Lawyers mitigate risk. It's their job to understand the law, make sure your company complies with regulations, and watch out for anything that could threaten the company or land you in court. Lawyers are not there to make your website friendly or soften difficult situations. As a writer, that's your job.

Even though you and your lawyer have different roles, your priorities don't have to conflict with each other. Here are some tips for working together on teams.

Start with policies, not semantics

Talk about the goals and policies you want to create. Figure out how your company will handle things if something goes wrong. Answer these questions together:

- What risk is the business facing? What do readers need to understand?
- How are readers expected to behave? What obligations do they have?
- What obligations does the business have? What promises are we making?
- How will the business handle user or customer data?

Get a bigger picture before you dive into the text itself. Once you know how you want to talk about your policies, find a good way to present the information.

Talk it through

If a particular paragraph or clause isn't working, bring it up with your lawyer and explain why it's overreaching or confusing. Explain how readers might feel at this point in the flow or reading experience. You may need to restate your goals, present copy options, or look at how other companies handle similar situations. Talk it out together, and find a happy medium between being safe and being clear.

Clarity above all

Watch out for boilerplate and standardized wording. If your legal team proposes language that you're uncomfortable with, offer an alternative in plain language. Think creatively about each piece of text until everything reads well. As much as possible, avoid legalese, jargon, and Latin phrases like *repudiation* or *ad litem*. If you don't immediately recognize a term, your readers probably won't either. Find out if you can replace those murky phrases with wording that's easier for people to understand.

As Justice Clarence Thomas says:

> What I tell my law clerks is that we write these [opinions] so that they are accessible to regular people. That doesn't mean that there's no law in it. There are simple ways to put important things in language that's accessible. As I say to them, the beauty, the genius is not to write a five-cent idea in a ten-dollar sentence. It's to put a ten-dollar idea in a five-cent sentence. That's beauty. That's editing. That's writing.[3]

Make sure each phrase is working hard to explain things, and don't forget to read your terms aloud to check that they're relatable.

---

3 Harvard Law School, "Justice Clarence Thomas Visits HLS," February 11, 2013, http://youtu.be/heQjKdHu1P4.

How Mandy Brown developed terms for humans

Mandy Brown is the cofounder and CEO of Editorially. Her company's policies and terms of service are written in plain English[1]—and shared with a Creative Commons license so others can repurpose them. We asked Mandy about her process and why she sees terms as an important part of the user experience.

"In many ways, this is the first bit of writing that anyone using our tool would come across," she says. "We felt like it was important to make a good impression. Good writing is something we care about." People tend to gloss over terms because it's not worth trying to read them. Mandy thinks that's by design, because the terms that are so poorly written tend to be the ones readers should be most concerned about. She says: "I want our users to read these things and have a sense of what they're getting themselves into, what kind of company we are, and what could happen later." That means explaining what will happen with people's work and data in plain language.

Before writing the terms, Mandy read through service documents from Google, Dropbox, GitHub, WordPress, Tumblr, and other companies that touch people's content, then wrote down what she liked and didn't like. She used that research to articulate Editorially's values before meeting with her lawyer, who drafted an original version of the terms. Then they worked on it back and forth. "If I did this again, I would start with my own copy and let our lawyer reword it," she says. "There are definitely some sentences in our terms where in retrospect they're not as accessible as I would like. But we have a lawyer who is very supportive of us doing this the right way—and that's a prerequisite."

Mandy considered including notes in Editorially's terms to summarize legalese wherever it was required, but she decided against that. She says, "If the legal boilerplate is confusing and the real English makes sense, but legally you're agreeing to the boilerplate—not to the annotations—there's a gap between what you're really agreeing to and what you might *think* you're agreeing to. It seems like if you can make it work in real English, then you should make it work in real English, and not have both."

---

1 http://stet.editorially.com/articles/writing-a-better-terms-of-service/

Use progressive disclosure

There will be times when you need to cover several concepts or legal disclosures at once. If you're concerned that will overwhelm readers, ask your legal counsel if there's anything that could be left out. Alternatively, you can propose breaking up the messages into digestible parts across several screens. This is called *progressive disclosure*, which is a technique used by ecommerce sites and other online services.[4] A common example is showing a shipping or return policy later in a checkout flow. Apps do similar things when you're signing up for an account or trying a new feature. This lightens the load for readers and helps them feel comfortable at each step in the process.

Find a way to present information that works for your company and your readers. Be ready to compromise from time to time. Every site has some legalese. Your goal is to improve the copy and help readers understand your service so there aren't any surprises.

Small updates over time

Keep your legal policies current. Like anything you write, legal documents take time, patience, and regular checkups. Listen for feedback and recurring themes from your customers. When things change, let people know in a timely manner. Some changes aren't that important—like fixing a typo or linking to another document—so have a plan for what's worth announcing and how you get the word out.

---

4 Jakob Nielsen, "Progressive Disclosure," Nielsen Norman Group, December 4, 2006, www.nngroup.com/articles/progressive-disclosure/.

Chapter Ten

MAKE IT FLOW

THINK ABOUT ALL OF THE ACTIONS people can take on your site. What do you ask them to do? Maybe you run a shop where customers can filter products by category, check out with a credit card, and post reviews. Or maybe you have a food blog where readers can comment on recipes, pin photos, and sign up for your newsletter. This chapter covers interface writing in detail. We'll show you how to improve:

- Signup, payment, and subscription flows
- Forms and prompts
- Product and feature tours
- Navigation links and search filters

These are the places where you ask people to participate in what you're doing. Your words can guide readers, bolster their decisions, and encourage them to take action. A friendly voice and clear information can make a big difference here. So let's start by defining flows more explicitly and exploring a few more examples.

The big picture

In Chapter 3: Make a Plan, we looked at how each piece of content on a website fits into a larger one. Paragraphs and images make sections; sections tie into features. All of these pieces come together to paint a bigger picture for readers.

Interface writing is the practice of developing text for applications, forms, and flows. This kind of writing is especially important for digital products and services, online publications, and mobile apps. But even if you don't see yourself as an interface writer, you work needs to fit into the interfaces on your site. Along with instructional text and images, interface content includes input fields, menus, links, buttons, labels, categories, and tags. On a larger team, you'll probably work closely with a designer and developer on these elements. As a writer, your job is to focus on the words themselves.

A *flow* is a series of screens that walks readers through a task. Thinking about your writing as part of a flow is useful because it puts the work in the context of what readers are trying to do. Each piece of text is part of a task, rather than a set of unrelated pages. When you write for interfaces, your words are there to support readers in whatever they're trying to do, whether that's making a purchase, learning something new, applying to a program, or connecting with a friend. Flows put you into the mindset of a clerk, tour guide, or customer service rep. Since you can't see your customers, you have to anticipate what they may need. If you can have a good conversation with them about what they're trying to do, they may be more interested in listening and paying attention.

Designer Frank Chimero says, "Every form is a question."[1] What questions are your forms and flows asking? How can you make them more meaningful? Websites ask people personal questions, tell them what to do with their time, and point them in a specific direction if they're taking a look around. Be kind and careful, and help readers make smart decisions. Flow implies moving forward steadily with unwavering focus. As a writer, you're here to help readers do just that.

1 Webstock '11, "Frank Chimero: The Digital Campfire," http://vimeo.com/22377758

Types of flows

Flows are common in online retail sites, mobile apps, and larger publications, like magazines and big newspapers. But they're important on simple sites, too. For example, if you run a blog with a newsletter, how do people sign up for it? Do you have a form on your site, or do you link to a newsletter service? If you're announcing an event, how do readers RSVP? Think about the different steps they take to give you their name and email address.

Another thing to think about is how people share images from your site to Pinterest, Twitter, or Facebook. Even if you're linking to another site, you can control part of that experience. Those are just a few examples to start with. Here are a few others, broken down into individual steps readers could take:

> *Read post → Click a link → View photo → Leave a comment*
>
> *Read post → View About page → Subscribe to email newsletter*
>
> *Search → Enter keywords → Filter by category, material, or brand → Choose a result → View details*
>
> *View App Store page → Read description → Download app → Read welcome → Sign up → Take product tour*
>
> *Read blog announcement → Shop → View item → Add to cart → Sign in or continue as guest → Enter billing and shipping info → Check out now*

Each of these flows has several branches, like decision points on a flowchart. For example, in the App Store flow you may need to sign in to download the app or update your credit card info. You could also come into a flow from different places, depending on whether a friend linked you to the page, you browsed the site yourself, or Google helped you with your search. You get the idea.

When you're working on an assignment, it's easy to get caught up in the details and forget your larger set of goals. Look at the writing as part of a larger story or puzzle. That'll help you see how everything fits together and help your website make sense. When you're refining part of a flow, think about the logical steps around it:

- What is the reader trying to do?
- What could the reader be feeling?
- How did the reader get here?
- What's happening next?
- What choices can they make?

Flows require you to figure out the big picture and refine even the smallest details in an interface. That means thinking big and small at the same time to meet readers where they are. There are a few ways to approach this.

Survey the area

Take an inventory of the flows on your site. Write down the most important actions people can take. Choose one flow to start with. For example, if you're a nonprofit, your donation flow is probably the best place to focus your attention at first.

Go through the flow, step by step, and make notes about the language you see. Write down the actions a reader would take, along with any buttons or links you have to click to move forward in the flow. Take a screenshot of each step. (There are lots of tools out there for taking full-length screenshots. You can also ask your design team for mock-ups, or take several smaller screenshots if that's easier.)

For Shortstack Books, you could start with a logical place where someone would hear about the shop and map the steps from there:

1. A post from a friend talking about the shop
2. The Shop page, which highlights books for sale

3. The Book page, which features a specific book and prompts the customer to add it to the cart

4. The Cart page, with a book in the cart

5. The Checkout page, which asks for billing and shipping information

6. A confirmation message thanking the customer

7. An email receipt with order details

Now, think about where a reader might branch off. Take a look at the sequence. What are the secondary actions on the screen? Maybe the customer has a gift card or wants to ship internationally. Or, maybe someone wants to read the return policy before placing an order. Take a note of these secondary actions. We'll come back to those in a little while.

After you gather screenshots and notes, put them all in one place. If you're working with long pages or screens, you may want to print each one on a separate piece of paper and tack them up so you can reference them in order. Pull the whole sequence together for yourself so you can see it as a longer, connected story. Look at each step like a frame in a storyboard:

- What's happening in this frame?
- How does it relate to the frames before and after it?
- Is it complete? What's missing from the story?
- Does everything sound like it came from the same place?

Usually, this high-level thinking is done by an editor. But as a web writer, you'll often need to take on an editing role, either for yourself or your clients and coworkers. In any creative field—design, visual arts, software development, filmmaking, cooking, or music, to name a few—thinking like an editor can help you tie everything together, put the pieces in the right place, and prep them for a public audience.

Capture the flow

When you're ready to make some changes, start small at first. You don't have to look at the copy in every branch or every flow at once. Pick one or two branches and start with those.

You may find it handy to make a master document to reference throughout the project. This will be especially useful if you're rewriting a complicated flow or developing a mobile app. Gather up the screenshots and start a new file in your favorite word processor. Make a table with three columns: (1) screenshots, (2) copy, and (3) notes. Don't worry about the styling. It can be quite plain (**Figure 10.1**).

FIGURE 10.1 Organize your screenshots, copy, and notes in one document.

In the first column, add the first screenshot from the flow. If you're working with sketches or wireframes, you can put them here instead of screenshots. In the second column, paste in the existing copy or write some placeholder copy. And in the third column, add notes for yourself and your team. You may have questions about how something behaves or how your legal team wants to talk about a feature. Put those in questions alongside the appropriate screen.

Add a new row for each step in the flow. Include secondary messages or branches if you want to review those too. As you work through each step in the flow, replace the existing or placeholder copy with what you want to say. You can also include multiple copy directions for discussion.

Setting up the flow like this can help you stay organized as you work through the writing and editing process. It will also help other people understand your process and the reasoning behind your content decisions.

Now that you have the screens together, let's look at the writing itself.

Develop a structure

Flows are great places to practice your editing skills. To start, read through the screens chronologically and think about the story arc. Does it make sense? Does each piece of content serve a purpose? If the reader needs to make a decision, ask yourself how the interface could clarify that and prompt them in a considerate way. Make sure each screen is working toward your goals. Then, clean up the structure by working through these considerations:

Order: Arrange the events with the most important information at the top. Cluster secondary elements together. Move details about next steps, related links, and share links off to the side or near the bottom. For a longer flow, group your questions and form fields into sections by topic. For example, on a checkout page, you could have sections for order details, billing info, shipping info, and gift options. Add clear headings so people can see where they are in the process.

Focus: Ask yourself what you want readers to do. Does the flow help them focus on the task at hand? Or are there any interruptions? Make sure your instructions are clear—tuck those ads and surveys out of the way. Narrow down the number of decisions readers have to make by limiting calls to action.

Timing: Think about what situation readers are in. Look at each part of the flow individually. Could this message alarm or confuse people? Or is this the right moment to prompt them to take action? Make sure each message is timely and relevant.

Pacing: Look at all of the topics you've covered. Is the information digestible? If you read it aloud, it is too fast or too slow? Could anything overwhelm readers or insult their intelligence? Help people learn at a comfortable pace. Strike a balance between setting clear expectations and staying out of the way.

As you review the flow, think of other ways you could encourage people to get through it. You may need to move things around or soften the language. Maybe the structure is solid, but you need to clarify why a particular feature matters, what it does, or why it's necessary to create an account. Again, think about how you might talk to someone in person about this issue. Help readers follow along, find what they need, and feel good about it in the process.

Remember that content doesn't solve everything. You may be dealing with a design problem, a business decision that isn't friendly to people outside the company, or part of a new feature that isn't fully developed. As a writer on the project, it's your job to pay attention to the text and think about how it relates to the rest of the experience. Stay in touch with your design and development team, especially when you find something that isn't working. Talk it out together to find the right solution for your readers.

The little things

As you review each part of the flow, think about the content you can't see. For example, does a particular screen trigger any error messages, emails, or notifications? What happens if the reader decides to unsubscribe or share this with a friend? Many companies overlook these little details, but they're an important part of your communications. Forms and confirmation messages often appear right at the moment when someone decides to take action or interact with your site. That's the perfect time to show you care and boost the reader's confidence.

Look back at the list of content types on your site. Gather up any messages that relate to the flow. You may need to ask a coworker to pull them from your codebase or content management system. In the meantime, read through your help center, training materials, technical documentation, and legal policies. Does everything sound like it came from your company? Make sure the smaller bits sound as good as the rest of your site.

Audit the words

One way to fine-tune a flow is to review the names of individual elements on your site. This is sometimes called a *nomenclature audit*. Think about the words you use to describe people, places, and tasks. What nouns and verbs do you use? The point of this exercise is think about the system of words you use in the ever-expanding galaxy of your website.

Let's look at an example for Shortstack Books. For the summer reading camps, we'll need nouns to describe people and places, and verbs to describe actions people can take. For instance, should people *register* for an event, *join* an event, or *RSVP*? What will we call attendees? They're not all kids. What about the people running the summer camp? We could have specific labels for camp counselors, volunteers, sponsors, teachers, and parents.

To review the terms on your site, open it up in your browser and start a new text file. Scan through the navigation links in the header, footer, menus, and sidebars. Write down every name and label you see. Look at the buttons and calls to action. Scroll through your landing pages and copy down those terms, too. For now, just list the names quickly as you see them. If it helps to group them by task or topic, you can do that as well.

When you finish making the list, scrutinize each word. Check for these qualities, along with voice and tone:

Clarity: Each term should be immediately understandable, even when it's taken out of context, and you should be able to guess where it goes. Avoid words that are vague or repetitive. If any term slows you down, consider rewriting it.

Effective over clever

Randy J. Hunt is the creative director at Etsy and the author of *Product Design for the Web*. For him, clarity is not only important, but also part of his personal style. He says, "Before I came to Etsy, we built this ecommerce marketplace called Supermarket, where we sold products made by designers. The tagline was: 'Great design straight from designers.' There's a *little* flavor there, but not much. It's about as blunt as it can be while still being friendly."

Randy favors clarity over cuteness, especially in web products and interface copy. "When I started at Etsy, a lot of things were cute or clever," he says. "In some cases, we were working against ourselves. We had great product concepts that were confusing because of how we chose to name or explain them. There was too much color or the words were too expressive. It felt like we were inventing cognitive load for people." He mentioned the Alchemy feature, which let visitors request custom items from Etsy sellers but has since been phased out.

In interface copy, there's not a lot of room to be cheeky. You may need to introduce a new concept or help readers through a tricky process. Frilly names and jazzy wording can slow readers down. Randy recommends saving the cutesy language for the right time. He says, "If a feature functions in some special way or is a distinct part of a product experience, it might warrant some extra special name because there's actually something different about it. Otherwise, it feels like you're trying too hard. That has its place in marketing, but not in UI copy."

For a shopping cart or signup form, don't feel pressure to be creative with the language. Think about what the reader is trying to do. Are there similar flows, buttons, or tasks on other websites? If so, don't reinvent the metaphors. Make sure your writing speaks to readers and their expectations. But if you're writing a landing page, blog post, or email campaign, it could be a good time to have a little fun.

Accuracy: Set good expectations. Should readers expect to "Read more" or "Learn more" on the next page? If readers ask for more results, will they "See more" or "See all" of the remaining results on the following page? Review each word to see if it's appropriate for the task or audience.

Consistency: Refer to the same thing in the same way each time. Terms should complement one another and feel like they belong to the same group or family. For example, do you ask people to "Sign in" and "Log out"? Keep the same perspective and mirror the language appropriately. Watch out for pluralizing inconsistently, too.

Distinctness: Make the terms different enough from one another so readers can tell them apart. If you have too many options, consider combining two of them. For example, if you're selling only a handful of jackets and coats, you could combine them into "Outerwear" or "Jackets and Coats" as a category.

Review each term with a critical eye. Hunt for gaps and inconsistencies. You'll probably find names or labels that need to be revised. You may have to add another word, look up alternate terms in a thesaurus, or work with your designer to fix the order of information. This exercise is a great way to ensure that readers have clear links and useful filters to help them find their way around your site.

Tie everything together

When you get to the end of the flow, think about what happens next. Writing is about making useful connections for readers, so build on the ideas you just covered. Include useful links or show the reader something new. If someone just bought tickets for a show, provide directions to the venue or say whether it's okay to bring a snack. On the Shortstack website, you could show other books that readers may like or tell them about upcoming events after they make a purchase. Point to things you'd share with friends if you were giving them a tour or guiding them through the process.

Does the flow have any dead ends? If so, consider pointing out a new feature or prompting the reader to subscribe. Tie related topics and flows together to keep the story going. Reread through the flow one more time. Look for any gaps in the information. If you were expecting a different level of detail, think about how you could balance it out.

Offer different paths

Choose Your Own Adventure books are written from a second-person perspective, so the reader takes on the role of the hero. When something happens or a decision needs to be made, the reader gets to choose from a handful of options—and each option leads to an alternate ending in the story. By writing different choices and branches into the story, the author makes room for the reader to become part of the narrative. This may be a useful metaphor as you think about expanding flows on your website. For instance, you may have a primary message that's really important but want to offer an alternate ending in a secondary message to encourage readers to stick around.

Let's work through a few examples. (These are messages, or information you could convey, not example copy.)

When viewing an article or image:

> Primary: Buy, bookmark, favorite, comment, or share this.
> Secondary: Sign up to post your own. Or browse similar results.

Before signing in:

> Primary: Welcome. Please sign in or create an account.
> Secondary: Reset your password to continue.

After downloading a new app:

> Primary: View or dismiss the tour.
> Secondary: See examples of a feature in action. Or read more about it on the blog or in the help center.

After signing out:

> Primary: You've signed out. Sign in again to continue.
>
> Secondary: Get help or report a problem. Or check out these new articles on the blog.

After unsubscribing from a newsletter:

> Primary: You've been unsubscribed.
>
> Secondary: Tell us why you unsubscribed. Or subscribe to our blog, or follow us on Twitter and Facebook.

Surfacing these secondary choices at the right time can delight readers and improve their overall experience.

Loop back

Review your copy when it's live on the site. Check for typos or spacing issues. Read through the flow in context, and look for awkward bumps or phrases. Remember to revisit related content, too. If you made changes to a product description, legal message, or navigational link, update the help content to reflect the changes. Keep everything updated as you improve your site.

Practice on another site

Another way to practice refining flows is to edit someone else's writing. Pretend that you're planning to buy a gift or pay a bill. Or download that app your friends keep talking about, and take screenshots of the App Store description, signup form, and introductory content. Think about how you could improve the structure and language of the information. To be fair, you probably won't know the business reasons that went into the writing itself, but you can practice thinking about what works and what doesn't. Taking a curious, critical stance as a reader will help you improve your own work.

Chapter Eleven

THE REVISION PROCESS

EDITING IS A HUGE PART of any writer's job. You need to gather feedback, proofread your own work, and revise other people's writing too. Editing is the single most important thing you can do to prepare your work for the web.

In this chapter, you'll learn how to:

- Share drafts in a courteous, efficient manner
- Incorporate feedback and revise your own writing
- Approach peer editing from a teaching perspective

These skills will help you polish your work and keep your projects running smoothly.

Handling drafts

In Chapter 4: Writing Basics, we shared tips for reviewing your work and keeping it concise. Now let's look at how to gather and incorporate feedback from other people.

Introduce it

The review process sets the tone for how you collaborate on the writing itself. We've talked about how important your readers are, but your colleagues are your first audience. Before you share a draft, consider your reviewers and their needs. Your reviewers could be editors, topical experts, coworkers, clients, early readers, and even friends. Make a plan for sharing drafts with them and soliciting their input.

Give some context

Think about what you're trying to accomplish with your draft, and set it up for your reviewers. In a few words, help them understand where you're coming from, what's in flux, or what questions you have. Call out style choices you made, particularly if there are exceptions to your style guide. If you're unsure about specific details or need more information, flag your questions inline.

Be succinct. If you find yourself writing more than a few paragraphs or bullets, consider setting up a meeting with your reviewers to discuss your questions ahead of time, instead of dropping them in with a draft.

If you're working on a long-term project, tell them where you are in the process. Is the draft sketchy, roughly halfway done, or almost ready for publication? Is it part of a larger set of content types? Give some context so you can have a productive conversation about the draft.

Choose a friendly format

Share your draft in a friendly format. Consider creating a text file in Markdown so your team can see the hierarchy without having to fight off invisible character monsters from your word processor. If you need to discourage people from arm-wrestling with you in Track Changes, don't share a draft in a Word document. You may find it easier to write in a Google Doc (with editing powers turned off but commenting left on), or in a PDF if you don't want line edits yet. Find the right format for your team—and remember that the goal for the first round of revisions is to talk about the ideas you want to convey, not the exact wording.

Tell people what kind of feedback you need

You can also avoid getting into back-and-forth discussions about sentence-level decisions by telling your team what kind of comments you want. We like to think in terms of high-level feedback and low-level feedback.

High-level feedback answers questions like these:

- Is it clear? Does it make sense?

- Does it flow? Are there places where you get lost?

- Does it cover the most important topics?

- Does anything insult your intelligence or go over your head?

- Are there places where you need a story or an example?

These are the questions that a developmental editor would answer when reviewing your work. High-level feedback is useful for keeping your draft on track and developing your writing early in the process.

Low-level feedback is more granular and includes comments on convoluted phrasing, confusing messages, misspellings, and grammatical errors. This is the kind of feedback a copy editor would give when reviewing a draft. It's no less important—and keeps your style consistent—but it's much more useful when you've already put your ideas down and are ready to polish them.

In any draft cycle, try to get both of these kinds of feedback, depending on where you are in the process. Just be sure to specify what you're asking for when you share your draft, whether that's a high-level read-through or detailed line edits.

Define roles and set deadlines

Make sure everyone in the review process knows what they need to do. Are you waiting for replies before you publish this—or will you post it at a specific time? Set clear roles, deadlines, and expectations. This is especially important if your draft is making the rounds with people outside your immediate project team. Sometimes it's as simple as picking a person and asking them for feedback by a specific time.

Generally speaking, it's easier to finalize a draft with a small number of people involved in the feedback loop. At a large company, you'll need to vet your drafts with more people than if you're working with clients or writing for yourself. You may want to select a few people as editors or approvers but keep others involved only as reviewers without giving them final say.

When things go awry

If you're going to miss a deadline, let people know. Tell your editor or reviewers the work is taking longer than expected. Maybe you need another day to finalize your draft, or you need to do more research to better understand your part of the assignment. Be specific, and don't make others follow up with you multiple times. Let them know you're working on it and tell them when to expect your reply.

If a reviewer is running behind, it's fine to nudge them by email—but do it nicely. After all, you work with these lovely people, and you want to have a good relationship with them. The same goes for people outside your company. When you're a writer, everyone is a potential client—so be professional every time you contact someone.

Taking in feedback

As you start receiving feedback, take some time to think about it and check it against your goals. If several people are reviewing your draft, give them time to weigh in before you start revising. People will naturally disagree with one another, and you may waste time if you jump in too soon. Here are some things to consider when you're looking at feedback and deciding whether to incorporate it.

Listen for the levels

Ask yourself if the feedback is high-level or low-level. That will help you decide what to do next. If it's a small change that clarifies your message, go ahead and make that revision. But if it's high-level feedback about the structure or meaning of the piece, you may need to do more research before going back to your draft. If the feedback starts heading in the wrong direction, you may need to politely restate your goals for the piece.

Talk it out

If you don't understand a comment or aren't sure how to apply it, talk to your reviewer about the suggestion. Solve the problem together. Use the feedback as a reason to have a meaningful discussion about the text. If you're going to ignore several comments from someone, you may want to explain why you're not incorporating those changes. Like your in-person communications, your writing should be built on trust and shared goals. So if you feel like you're constantly at odds with your editor or reviewers, you may need to step back and do some interviews again or refine your editorial process.

Appreciate it

Keep in mind that feedback is a gift, not an insult. Don't think of your reviewers' comments like marks on a term paper. You're not in trouble, you're working together—and your reviewers want to help make your ideas clear to your readers. Thank them for their time and their comments, even if you decide not to incorporate some of their suggestions.

Let it rest

Give yourself time to reflect on a draft before publishing it. If you can let your writing sit overnight, the next morning is a great time to send it out for review. Of course, there will be times when you need to write something and get it out very quickly, especially in emergencies. But if you have to publish it in the next hour, ask one or two people to spot-check it first.

Give it another read-through

When you think your draft is finished, give it one more read-through to make sure your tone flows with your overall communication style. Check for the basics: Is it clear? Is it friendly? Is it useful? If you haven't added subheadings or a title, do that now. And remember to read it aloud to make sure it sounds like you.

Good is good enough

You're going to mess up from time to time—mistakes are part of the writing process. You'll forget to fix a typo or change some wording around, even if someone flagged it ahead of time. Or you'll forget to loop someone in on a draft. Most writers put a lot of pressure on themselves to get things right the first time. But you're human, and nobody's perfect. You're writing for the web, so for the most part, you'll be able to fix things after they go live.

That said, polish your writing as much as possible before putting it out there. Recruit some early readers—and offer to be an early reader for others.

When you're the editor

As writers, we often get to switch places with teammates and take on the role of the editor. This is a great time to think about your house style and listen for common questions. Try to approach editing like a teacher. Center your work around your teammates, their skill levels, and what's important for your company to communicate.

As an editor, you take on the voice of the reader. You read, review, reorganize, revise, and reflect on what's being said from an outside perspective. Make the content manageable for your audience, and show your team how that works.

Editorial etiquette

Here are few ways to be helpful when you're reviewing or editing someone else's work.

Say what you need up front

You may know more about your publishing process than your contributing authors. Tell them everything they need to know up front. If you have a style guide or specific guidelines, share those ahead of time. If a piece needs specific accompaniments, like an author bio, illustrations, or captions, spell that out early in the writing process. Set clear deadlines and help your contributors get everything together on time.

Ask before overhauling it

Before you get your hands dirty and rewrite someone else's draft, ask permission to make significant changes. Not everyone has a thick skin when it comes to their writing. Writers will be more likely to accept your feedback if they feel like they're part of the editing process.

Give good feedback

When you're passing back a draft, summarize what you've changed. If any text needs rewriting, help the writer understand why you think so. Don't just cite rules and leave it at that. Explain how you think about style and which guidelines you're referencing. Acknowledge good work too. This is especially important if you're working with newer writers, who may need some encouragement along the way. Be specific in your comments, and include language suggestions where it's useful.

Look for themes

Watch out for recurring issues and themes as you edit. If you see a writer making the same mistake repeatedly or notice several people making a similar one, think about how to teach them a better way. Mention your style guide gently when it's appropriate. And if your style guide doesn't cover that recurring issue, it's probably time to update it.

In all of your communications—from interviews and conversations, to writing and revising drafts, to teaching others about your style—the goal is to get closer to the truth for your readers and your business. So keep pushing and find a way to make it fun for your team.

Write beside them

Here are a few ways to teach writers about voice and tone, and build on your style.

Don't kill their voice

Be careful when revising someone else's sentences. Don't overedit things and squash the author's voice. As an editor, your job is to help the reader understand what's being said, not to be the ultimate style enforcer. If a sentence reads well but doesn't sound like something you'd say, ask yourself whether your edits reflect your personal preference or whether it truly needs to be rewritten to sound more like the company. If a writer needs help finding the right voice, refer to your voice and tone guidelines and talk about it together.

Show them what works

If a writer is having trouble applying a style decision, suggest a few options that work and explain the structure behind them. Maybe a sentence is too long and clumsy unless you go with a dependent clause. Or maybe you need to use the passive voice here to make it softer. Help your team understand your larger goals for the content; those guiding principles are more effective than telling them to look back at rule 32.

Be willing to negotiate

Style decisions are not a matter of right and wrong. There will be times when you need to make exceptions to your homegrown rules. Be willing to talk about what makes sense for a particular article, piece, or situation. As Arthur Plotnik says, "I have seen too many editors search through piles of back issues to determine 'how have we done it in the past.'... I tell my editors to be consistent within the present issue and, when we have the time, we will work up a style rule based on good sense—not precedent."[1]

---

1 Arthur Plotnik, *The Elements of Editing* (New York: Macmillan, 1982), 3.

Refine your process

Continue developing your editorial process as you work through drafts and reviews. If you hire more writers, take on new content types, or add new technology behind the scenes, remember to revisit your goals and your readers' needs accordingly.

Your refinements may be large or small. You might need to edit your style guide or set up more regular check-ins with reviewers. Or you might want to speed up the beginning of each project with a template or list of questions. Even if you work at a big publishing company, you can expect your role and editorial process to change once in a while. Whatever your situation, try to keep it simple.

Chapter Twelve

STYLE GUIDES

SO FAR, WE'VE SHARED EXERCISES for improving your writing and developing your style. But your job doesn't end there. Share what you've learned so your team can preserve your hard work.

This chapter will guide you through defining your house style and teaching your team to work with it. You'll learn how to:

- Develop and maintain a useful style guide
- Give people the tools they need to write well
- Workshop copy ideas as a group
- Evolve your house style as your company grows

These tips will help you create an environment where voice and tone are on people's minds. Let's work through the process of putting your style into words.

Define your style

You need a style guide. It doesn't have to be exhaustive. We recommend keeping it brief, easy to update, and even easier to reference. Once you've established a few standards for your content, making a style guide is a relatively straightforward task.

Show them the way

A style guide helps writers understand your brand voice and content standards. It's a living, working guide to writing for your website. Here are a few ways it can be of service.

Keep things consistent. Consistent language and wording make your content more polished and authoritative. Whether you spell out state names or use postal abbreviations isn't a matter of right or wrong, but you should pick one and stick with it. A style guide helps you define those terms and spelling choices for your team.

Create clarity. A style guide can highlight content goals, terms to avoid, and common language mistakes. By clarifying your standards, a style guide helps you create clarity in your communications.

Save time. A style guide can answer questions people didn't know they had and keep things moving when you're not available. It can also settle small stylistic disagreements without getting an editor or emotions involved.

Empower writers. People feel more comfortable writing when they have a reference to lean on. Think of it like a car manual: you might not use it every day, but it's helpful to have around when questions come up. A style guide makes it possible to formalize everyday editorial decisions, share them with others, talk about them, and evolve them over time.

Teach voice and tone. Your style guide is a compass for your company's voice and tone. It helps writers understand your brand and your writing principles. And it guides their decisions about intonation and word choice for specific types of content.

A compass, not a remedy

A style guide can help you train and support writers as they learn to self-edit, but it shouldn't stand alone. Here's a summary of what a style guide is *not*.

It's not a workbook. Treat your style guide as a reference, not a cure-all. Don't expect it to fix sloppy writing or solve all of your content problems. It's there so you can point to it, but you'll still need to help people be clear and friendly in their writing.

It's not for everyone. Some people on your team won't need to use your style guide. Don't try to force it on your CEO, for example. It won't replace an editor, so build in time to fix errors during the review process.

It's not a bible. Don't put too much stock in your style guide. It's an important tool that can improve your content, but you'll need to refine it over time. And you may need to make exceptions once in a while—we'll discuss that later in this chapter.

Start with a solid foundation

There are plenty of great books on style out there. There's no point in rewriting them yourself. Before you make a style guide from scratch, think about what your team needs to improve their writing.

For most teams, it makes sense to pick an existing style guide as a foundation and build on it. In this section, we'll share some foundational style guides and show you how to make your own style guide to complement it.

The Elements of Style
Strunk and White's classic is perfect for bloggers and companies who need a lightweight, accessible guide to writing. It's a must-read for any writer, but it might be too concise for your needs. It doesn't cover internet-specific topics, so digital companies that go this route will have a lot to cover in their own style guides.

The Yahoo! Style Guide
We recommend Yahoo's style guide for most companies, especially those in the tech world. It was created for people who publish digital content, so it covers topics like headers, email, and even SEO. It's practical, well organized, and easy to flip through.

The Chicago Manual of Style

Published since 1906 by the University of Chicago Press, *The Chicago Manual of Style* is still widely used by publishers, tech companies, and other industries. It's comprehensive—so much so that it can be difficult to navigate. This one is more of an expert's tool. While it's handy for editorially minded people and covers topics you might not find elsewhere, you wouldn't want to plop this on an engineer or support rep's desk.

The Economist Style Guide

The Economist created this guide for journalists, but it's useful for any company that publishes information. It's rigorous, practical, and more compact than some of the other guides out there. It focuses on the reader, with tips like: "Do not be too pleased with yourself," and "Use the language of everyday speech, not that of spokesmen, lawyers or bureaucrats." If you have international readers, you might enjoy the entries on idioms, foreign names, and Americanisms.

AP Stylebook

Associated Press style is used primarily in news writing, but this is a good guide for any publisher to have on hand. It favors simplicity, which is also useful for copywriters.

Flip through these foundational guides and find the one that fits your needs. Pick one that's close to your house style so you don't have to rewrite all the rules in it. It may help you to write down the most important rules and style decisions beforehand so you can compare notes.

There are plenty of other style guides out there, like the *MLA Handbook for Writers of Research Papers* and the *Publication Manual of the American Psychological Association*. MLA and APA style are more appropriate for academic writing, so if you're a copywriter, you can probably leave these on the shelf.

Buy a few copies of your foundational style guide, or get an online subscription for your team. Use it as a reference to teach people grammar basics and general guidelines, like how to use commas and write good headlines. By starting with a more comprehensive reference, you can keep your own style guide brief and focused. Let's work through that part now.

Consider your audience

Figure out who's going to read your style guide and rely on it regularly. Is it a small group, or will you distribute it to several different teams? Does your audience consist of professional writers and editors? Or are they subject-matter experts who may not consider themselves writers? Or maybe it's just for you for now—that's okay too. Thinking about your audience will help you decide what to cover and how much detail to include.

If your style guide is for experienced writers and editors, you probably don't need to explain grammar basics. For example, you could get away with saying "use the Oxford comma" or "use the serial comma," without having to explain that it's the comma after the second-to-last item in a list. But for a wider audience of writers, you probably need to include specific examples with each entry to clarify your style choices.

Components

No two style guides are exactly alike. Yours will be informed by internal conversations, questions from contributors, design critiques, and problems you see regularly. The next few sections cover topics you may want to include depending on what you publish, who's going to use the guide, and which guide you chose as a foundation.

Principles

Include a few overarching content principles so your team understands the spirit of your style guide. Give an overview of what you're trying to accomplish with your content. If you only have a minute to tell writers what they need to know, what would you say? Put that here.

If you have brand guidelines, design attributes, or general principles for your communications, you can use those as your content principles. As an example, here are the design principles from GOV.UK's style guide:

1. Start with needs.
2. Do less.
3. Design with data.
4. Do the hard work to make it simple.
5. Iterate. Then iterate again.
6. Build for inclusion.
7. Understand context.
8. Build digital services, not websites.
9. Be consistent, not uniform.
10. Make things open: it makes things better.[1]

These principles apply to writers, editors, and designers—and complement their content style guide.[2]

If your brand standards focus on visual design and the use of your company's logo, you'll need to write more specific content principles that cover the writing itself. These should align with your mission and complement your brand standards. Here are some examples:

Be kind.	Be honest.
Keep it brief.	Build trust.
Write how you speak.	

Keep this section concise and put it near the top of your guide. Do what you can to help people understand your style before getting into the details.

Voice and tone

Define your style and say how you're different. Dig into your company's personality and include tips for striking the right tone. If you made a

---

1 GOV.UK Government Digital Service, "Design Principles," https://www.gov.uk/design-principles.
2 GOV.UK Government Digital Service, "Content Style Guide," https://www.gov.uk/design-principles/style-guide.

This But Not That list (refer to Chapter 5: Find Your Voice), include it as a reference. This is also a great place to call out distinctive style decisions, like how you talk to readers or how you use pronouns.

Content types

List all of the content types your company publishes (refer to Chapter 3: Make a Plan for a full list). Sort them alphabetically, or try to loosely reflect the order in which people encounter them on your website. Name each content type (blog post, help document, marketing campaign, signup form) and include a few specifics about how to write them. Your voice and tone standards should carry through each of these, so think about how writers can bring your style to life in those moments. Give examples and explain how they work. You could also contrast good examples with bad ones to illustrate your thinking.

If you have several guidelines for each of your content types, include a section for each entry. Here's an example of what that could look like for Shortstack Books:

> **Blog post**
>
> Purpose: Encourage people to shop in the online store or visit us in person. Share our excitement about new arrivals and in-store exclusives. Announce upcoming in-store events and summer reading camps. Promote reading, literacy, and the larger community of children's book collectors.
>
> Readers: Frequent customers who love our shop, potential customers, and especially parents and children's book collectors
>
> Average length: 250–1,200 words

If your site has similar content types, include links to examples or screenshots as visual aids so people can tell them apart. Help writers see the subtle differences between the content types. Remember to keep the images and samples updated as your website changes.

You may also want to make a larger section for a content type that you can pull out as a reference. For example, maybe you have a lot of blog contributors, but those people don't need to understand your other content standards. In that case, include a section called "Writing for the blog" that you can share separately. Give writers what they need without wasting their time or diluting the message.

Grammar and usage

Keep this section focused on guidelines that are specific to your company. These could include standards for capitalization, abbreviations, acronyms, and other words you want to emphasize. If you make exceptions to the rules in your foundational guide, include those too.

Specify whether you use the Oxford comma, whether to use contractions, when to hyphenate, and when to spell out numbers or use numerals—especially if any of these choices conflict with your foundational guide. For a magazine or news site, you may want to tell writers how to introduce people (usually first and last name) and how to reference them after that (first or last name). You could also set standards for sources or footnotes.

A list of common words can show writers how to spell and capitalize product names. It can also quickly clear up confusion between "login" (a noun or adjective) and "log in" (a verb). If you avoid specific industry terms or jargon like "below the fold" or "digerati," put those in there too.

Alphabetize your list of grammar and usage guidelines so people can skim to the right section. Remember, don't try to make it exhaustive. If a writer can look something up in a dictionary, it probably doesn't need to go in your style guide. For example, the differences between "further" and "farther" or "affect" and "effect" don't belong there, unless those happen to be words your company uses (or misuses) regularly.

Web style

Web style could be a subsection of your usage guidelines or a section of its own. If your team needs help organizing and styling text, make a note of that too. Here are a few things to include:

- Titles, headers, and subheaders
- Block elements, like block quotes, lists, or code snippets

- Image titles, caption length, alt text, and sizes
- Text styles: emphasis, italics, footnotes, and so on
- Keywords to use, like *bookshop, bookstore,* and *young readers*

Help your team keep these elements consistent by showing how to format them.

Resources

Wrap up your style guide with a brief list of resources for people who want to learn more about writing. Include a link to your foundational style guide, along with any other books or links that will help your team on a daily basis. (See the Further Reading section for our favorites.)

When you're done creating your style guide, read through it and make sure it's as brief as possible. Break it down into manageable chunks with clear, clickable headings. If people are overwhelmed at the sight of it, they won't take the time to read it. Make sure it's useful for your team and ask them for feedback.

Keep it fresh

All done? Awesome! Share your style guide and keep it updated. Don't let it gather dust on your desktop. Instead of making it a PDF, publish it somewhere that's easy to update and access. If your team uses a wiki, website, Google Docs, or GitHub, those are great places to start. If people are more comfortable with a link they can bookmark, make it a webpage. It doesn't have to be pretty, but it should be useful and treated as an important part of your communications. Like any living document, a style guide needs regular care and feeding, so make it easy to find and update.

Put someone in charge of the content in your style guide. If that's your job, keep it fresh and refer to it regularly. At a small company, you may be able to make edits on the spot. If that's not realistic, collect feedback over time and work the updates into your editorial calendar. Quarterly updates will keep it from going stale.

Treat your style guide as a supportive document, not a replacement for editorial thinking. When you're fielding questions or editing something, point to the appropriate section for more details. Offer to answer any questions or talk through the usage guideline for that topic. Help your team understand how to put your house style into action. If you find yourself explaining a style decision in a different way or offering examples by email, consider updating your style guide to reflect how you talk about it.

Spread the word

Now that you have a style guide, people can use it as a first line of defense when they have questions or need help with an assignment. But if you're an editor or in charge of a website, your job is to help people publish good content for your readers. That means teaching them about writing every chance you get.

Show and tell

Just like you sell your products and your company to customers, you need to promote your style internally too. Let people know about your brand, voice, and tone guidelines—and tell them how to reach you if they need help.

Make a presentation

In some organizations, a presentation is a great way to talk about style. You may want to share your style guide with a team of developers or designers. Or you may want to give new employees a brief orientation on your writing principles. A lecture-style talk is useful for introducing yourself and your team, especially if you're part of an editorial group at a larger company. Give yourself enough time to explain what you do, outline your content standards, and touch on important content types or tips you want everyone to know. Leave time at the end for questions.

How Facebook workshops ideas

In the past few years, Facebook's content strategy team grew to over 25 people. To keep up with growth, they started *flash*, or casual meetings to workshop ideas. Content strategy director Alicia Dougherty-Wold told us how flash supports the company's goals and editorial style.

Alicia says flash started early in the team's history: "We wanted to make sure we were all writing in the same voice and the easiest way to do this was to show each other work and talk about it." Since then, Facebook has defined content standards and formalized their voice. But flash is still a big part of the process. "It's equal parts writing workshop, design critique, content QA, and kaffeeklatsch," she says. "We use this time together to keep our product voice consistent across all the parts of Facebook, to stay aligned on content best practices and patterns, and to build camaraderie within our team." Alicia says flash works best with five to seven people—and unlike a formal critique, everyone participates.

Flash happens a few times a week, and content strategists drop in at a time that fits their schedule. Each person brings a draft and asks for specific kinds of feedback. Maybe they want to brainstorm ideas or share copy directions. Or maybe they need help finding a better way to say something. Alicia says, "No matter what you bring in, you feel like it gets better through the team's questions and suggestions."

Alicia adds, "We also participate in design critiques and collaborate with user experience research to make sure we get a wide range of feedback from people outside our team—especially from the people who'll use what we make." The team also does more structured editing passes, but they keep flash in the mix. She says, "We're an unusual content strategy team in that we do high-level strategic work and also the practical work of product and marketing writing and editing. It doesn't matter how long we've been in the field or worked at Facebook—we all want to keep learning from each other—and we do!"

Host office hours

Office hours are a common practice in colleges, where you can make an appointment with a professor outside of class. This gives you a chance to work on your assignment by yourself and then check in privately with your professor to make sure you're on the right track. You can do something similar with your colleagues. Set a time for them to meet with you individually and ask you style questions or work through a draft. You could also host group office hours where you help more than one person at a time. It may be useful for different writers to hear how you talk through style decisions with other people at your company.

Develop it together

Even if you're in charge of your style guide, the standards themselves should be an ongoing conversation with your team.

Start a style group

At a larger company or publication, you may want to form an official group for people who are interested in editorial decisions. Consider hosting a meeting once a quarter to answer questions in an open forum and talk about how your style is evolving. Ask your team if any of the guidelines are confusing or conflicting with each other. Include other people in the decision-making process. Give them a chance to learn how you settle discrepancies or prioritize changes.

Announce changes

Tell people about important changes. A *changelog*, or list of recent changes, may be useful at the end of your style guide. The *New York Times* does a great job of announcing style changes on their After Deadline blog.[3] The editorial staff posts updates about their stylebook, along with the reasoning behind specific changes. This helps everyone understand what's new and why the changes were made. Announcing style changes is especially important for publications and media organizations where everyone is invested in the house style.

---

3 Philip B. Corbett, "The Latest Style," *After Deadline,* October 29, 2013, http://afterdeadline.blogs.nytimes.com/2013/10/29/the-latest-style/.

AFTERWORD

WE WRAPPED UP THIS BOOK on a crisp April morning. It was a lot like any other day in the life of a web writer. We passed emails back and forth, collaborated on a draft, talked about open questions, renamed a few things, and revised sentences that weren't reading well. We went through each section of each chapter until it felt close enough.

And that's what we hope you've gleaned from this book. To think of writing as a process. To read your work aloud and talk about it with someone who cares as much as you do. To ask questions of yourself and your colleagues. To check in with your feelings as you write. To consider your voice and watch your tone. And to put your readers first.

You have what you need to do that. You know your mission, your goals, and your readers. You've established a friendly style, and you know how it fits within your different content types. You're already writing with style and purpose. So keep at it.

We can't wait to read your work.

ACKNOWLEDGMENTS

Thanks to Erin Kissane, for encouraging us to work together and for being a great influence.

To Alvin Diec, for reading our minds, designing the cover, and making us look good.

To Andrew Thomas Lee, for taking our portraits and making us laugh.

To Mark DiCristina, for invaluable feedback and support.

To the New Riders crew: Nancy Peterson, Margaret Anderson, Tracey Croom, Gretchen Dykstra, Mimi Heft, Kim Scott, Liz Welch, and Rebecca Plunkett—and to Michael Nolan who originally accepted our proposal. Thanks for making this possible.

To our contributors: Gabrielle Blair, Margot Bloomstein, Mandy Brown, Tiffani Jones Brown, Alicia Dougherty-Wold, Kristina Halvorson, Randy J. Hunt, Jodi Leo, Benjamin Lotan, Sarah Richards, and Corey Vilhauer. Thanks for sharing your time and your wisdom.

To our early readers: Britta Alexander, Vivian Bencich, Christopher Blizzard, Scott Boms, Mandy Brown, Deb Chachra, Vanessa Gennarelli, Lesley Graham, Roberto Greco, Richard Ingram, Diana Kimball, Jen Lowe, Rachael Maddux, Corey Mahoney, Stewart McCoy, Kenny Meyers,

Chelsea Randall, Austin Ray, Rachel Stevenson, Allen Tan, Nicholas Van Exan, Allyson Van Houten, Aarron Walter, and Bernard Yu, who gave insightful feedback and hearty encouragement on early drafts. We promise to return the favor.

And to Jack Cheng, Frank Chimero, Paul Ford, John Foreman, Ethan Marcotte, Samin Nosrat, and Khoi Vinh for early advice on the process.

Kate says:

Thanks to Nicole for being a wonderful writing partner and friend, and for keeping this project in line.

Thanks to Mark DiCristina, Ben Chestnut, Aarron Walter, and the whole team at MailChimp for teaching me so much, encouraging me to share the work we do together, and giving me time and space to write. And to Neil Bainton for hiring me in the first place. I sure love my job.

To Austin Ray and Rachael Maddux, my first editors. To my editors at *Forbes*, *A List Apart*, *UX Magazine*, Design*Sponge, and everyone else who lets me write. To Kristina Halvorson, Erik Westra, and Team Confab for taking a chance on me several years ago.

To the Reillys, the Kiefers, and the Lees. And to Andy, my favorite person in the whole entire universe.

Nicole says:

Thanks to Kate, for going all-in on this project and being a fantastic partner in the writing process. It's been a joy and an honor.

To Scott Boms, Tiffani Jones Brown, Sara Distin, Daniel Eizans, Bobby George, Roberto Greco, Jonathan Kahn, Erin Kissane, Rachel Lovinger, Megan Ma, Peter Richardson, Timothy Willis Sanders, Adam Schragin, Michael Seidel, Jesse Taggert, Dorian Taylor, Amy Thibodeau, Erik Westra, and anyone whose name I've missed: thank you for encouraging me to write.

Acknowledgments

To my clients and my former colleagues at Apple, Mule Design, Lab Zero, and Facebook: you make the web a warmer place.

To Dad, the Kennedys, and the rest of them Joneses.

To Debra and C&E for teaching me to look up and out.

To Joan, Janet, and Albie for lasagne and steak.

And to Max for dancing into my life at just the right time. I love you the world.

FURTHER READING

In this book, we focused on topics that apply to your daily work as a web writer or small business owner. The following books and resources cover related fields in more detail—from inspirational writing guides to specific topics like content strategy, web design, usability, and legal contracts. For more resources, visit http://nicelysaid.co.

Writing

Natalie Goldberg. *Writing Down the Bones: Freeing the Writer Within.* Boston: Shambhala, 2005.

Verlyn Klinkenborg. *Several Short Sentences About Writing.* New York: Vintage, 2012.

Anne Lamott. *Bird by Bird: Some Instructions on Writing and Life.* New York: Anchor, 1994.

Mary Pipher. *Writing to Change the World.* New York: Riverhead, 2006.

Dani Shapiro. *Still Writing: The Perils and Pleasures of a Creative Life.* New York: Atlantic Monthly Press, 2013.

Marjorie E. Skillin. *Words into Type.* Third edition. Englewood Cliffs, NJ: Prentice Hall, 1974.

Style

Chris Barr and The Senior Editors of Yahoo!. *The Yahoo! Style Guide: The Ultimate Sourcebook for Writing, Editing, and Creating Content for the Digital World*. New York: St. Martin's Griffin, 2010.

The Chicago Manual of Style Online. www.chicagomanualofstyle.org.

The Economist Style Guide. http://www.economist.com/styleguide/.

Peter Elbow. *Vernacular Eloquence: What Speech Can Bring to Writing*. New York: Oxford, 2012.

Patrick J. Lynch and Sarah Horton. *Web Style Guide*. Third edition. www.webstyleguide.com/wsg3/.

William Strunk Jr. and E.B. White. *The Elements of Style*. Fourth edition. New York: Longman, 2000.

William Zinsser. *On Writing Well*. Seventh edition. New York: Collins, 2006.

Editing

Claire Kehrwald Cook. *Line by Line: How to Edit Your Own Writing*. Boston: Houghton Mifflin Harcourt, 1985.

Scott Norton. *Developmental Editing: A Handbook for Freelancers, Authors, and Publishers*. Chicago and London: University of Chicago Press, 2009.

Arthur Plotnik. *The Elements of Editing: A Modern Guide for Editors and Journalists*. New York: Macmillan, 1982.

Carol Fisher Saller. *The Subversive Copy Editor: Advice from Chicago (or, How to Negotiate Good Relationships with Your Writers, Your Colleagues, and Yourself)*. Chicago: University of Chicago, 2009.

Research

Wayne C. Booth, Gregory G. Colomb, and Joseph M. Williams. *The Craft of Research*. Third edition. Chicago: University of Chicago Press, 2008.

Erika Hall. *Just Enough Research*. New York: A Book Apart, 2013.

Steve Portigal. *Interviewing Users: How to Uncover Compelling Insights*. New York: Rosenfeld Media, 2013.

Kio Stark. *Don't Go Back to School: A Handbook for Learning Anything*. Greenglass, 2013.

Content strategy

Margot Bloomstein. *Content Strategy at Work: Real-World Stories to Strengthen Every Interactive Project*. New York: Morgan Kaufmann, 2012.

Kristina Halvorson and Melissa Rach. *Content Strategy for the Web*. Second edition. Berkeley, CA: New Riders, 2012.

Erin Kissane. *The Elements of Content Strategy*. New York: A Book Apart, 2011.

Karen McGrane. *Content Strategy for Mobile*. New York: A Book Apart, 2012.

Sara Wachter-Boettcher. *Content Everywhere: Strategy and Structure for Future-Ready Content*. Brooklyn, NY: Rosenfeld Media, 2012.

Design

Dan M. Brown. *Communicating Design: Developing Web Site Documentation for Design and Planning*. Second edition. Berkeley, CA: New Riders, 2011.

Jason Fried. "Questions I Ask When Reviewing a Design." *Signal v. Noise,* October 11, 2011. http://37signals.com/svn/posts/3024-questions-i-ask-when-reviewing-a-design.

Randy J. Hunt. *Product Design for the Web: Principles of Designing and Releasing Web Products*. New Riders, 2014.

Mike Monteiro. *Design Is a Job*. New York: A Book Apart, 2012.

Jakob Nielsen and Don Norman. *Writing for the Web*. www.nngroup.com/topic/writing-web/.

Business and marketing

Clayton M. Christensen. *The Innovator's Dilemma: The Revolutionary Book that Will Change the Way You Do Business*. Reprint edition. New York: HarperBusiness, 2011.

Eric Karjaluoto. *Speak Human: Outmarket the Big Guys by Getting Personal*. Smashlab, 2009.

Austin Kleon. *Show Your Work! 10 Ways to Share Your Creativity and Get Discovered*. New York: Workman Publishing, 2014.

Youngme Moon. *Different: Escaping the Competitive Herd*. New York: Crown Business, 2010.

Marty Neumeier. *Zag: The Number One Strategy of High-Performance Brands*. Berkeley, CA: New Riders, 2007.

Legal writing

Bryan A. Garner. *Legal Writing in Plain English*. Second edition. Chicago: University of Chicago, 2001.

Tina L. Stark. *Drafting Contracts: How and Why Lawyers Do What They Do*. New York: Aspen Publishers, 2007.

Terms of Service; Didn't Read. http://tosdr.org.

INDEX